Outside the Ivory Tower:

A Guide for Academics Considering Alternative Careers

Outside the *Ivory* Tower:

A Guide for Academics Considering Alternative Careers

Margaret Newhouse, Ph.D.

❧

Office of Career Services
Faculty of Arts and Sciences
Harvard University

BIO

Margaret Locke Newhouse (Ph.D. in Political Science from UCLA) has counseled graduate students and Ph.D.'s at Harvard's Office of Career Services since 1989. She came to this position from a career in education, which includes high school teaching, university and college teaching (UCLA and Scripps College), directing internship programs (Wellesley and Scripps Colleges) that integrated the worlds of academia and work, and coordinating the RAND/UCLA Center for the Study of Soviet International Behavior. She has also been a volunteer community mediator for several years.

© 1993 by the President and Fellows of Harvard College
All rights reserved
Printed in the United States of America
10 9 8 7 6 5 4 3 2 1

Office of Career Services
Faculty of Arts and Sciences
54 Dunster Street
Harvard University
Cambridge, MA 02138
(617) 495-2595

ISBN 0-943747-08-2

Table of Contents

Acknowledgments

It has been my privilege over the past three and a half years to be a "co-explorer" with many Harvard graduate students and Ph.D.'s seeking alternatives to academic careers. The concerns and experiences they have shared in individual counseling sessions and in my extended workshops on Exploring Nonacademic Careers have both educated me and enriched this book. They have my heartfelt appreciation.

So, too, the many alumni of the Graduate School of Arts and Sciences (GSAS) who have so generously shared their stories and counsel—in conversations in their offices, over lunch, on the phone, through their participation in panels and workshops at the Office of Career Services (OCS), and through letters and other written materials. Their examples give this guide its special tone and greatest value, and their advice and support as Career Advisers has immeasurably aided many current academic career changers.

I am also indebted to many colleagues for their invaluable help all along the way. Marty Leape, Director of the Office of Career Services, has given support and astute advice from the beginning of the project. Judy Kugel, Director of the Office of Career Services at the Kennedy School of Government and Ilene Rudman, Counselor at Radcliffe Career Services, gave the first draft very close and perceptive readings and provided moral support for the project; Judy also critiqued the penultimate draft.

I benefited as well from editorial and substantive comments from Deborah Melone, Documentation Manager at Bolt Beranek and Newman Inc., Elizabeth Reed, Associate Director of the M.I.T. Office of Career Services, Andrew Ceperley of the Career Planning and Placement Office at the University of Virginia, and GSAS alumni Rob Scheinerman (Economics), Bob Hewes (Applied Sciences), and Sarah Chayes (History). Many of the individuals profiled in the text, as well as several graduate students in my workshops, have also made helpful suggestions.

Karen From has my everlasting appreciation for her conscientious, meticulous, and sensitive editing and production oversight. Paul Bohlmann spontaneously designed the cover and gave other valuable design advice; and Susan Vacca cheerfully provided essential advice and assistance, especially with the Bibliography. Karin Powell and Eileen Farren provided indispensible administrative assistance and typing/production help with the graphs, tables, resumes, and manuscript. Thanks are also due to Lisa Wentz for her thorough proofreading and helpful suggestions, to Lisa Muto for last-minute editing advice, and to work-study students Victor Chang and Ramin Toloui for help with the Bibliography and charts.

For their indirect support, heartfelt thanks go to Joseph P. Newhouse and Eric and David Newhouse.

Introduction

A decade ago this book would have been both more heretical and even more necessary than it is today. More necessary because the dismal academic job market—even worse than today's—left many graduate students and new Ph.D.'s little choice but to seek nonacademic jobs; and more heretical because, despite the grim market forces, few established academics wanted to acknowledge career possibilities outside the ivory tower.

Despite predictions of a reviving academic job market in the mid-to-late 1990s,[1] many of today's graduate students and younger professors are considering alternative careers. Some have discovered in graduate school that they are less suited to the academic life than they initially thought, as their interests and values have changed, or as firsthand professional experience has proved distasteful. Others have become discouraged by the still depressed academic job market, which continues to defy optimistic predictions; still others are constrained by their spouses' careers and/or other family considerations. Some Ph.D.'s have burned out after a partial "career" in academia (often marked by part-time, temporary positions); others may be affected by the increasing frequency of mid-career changes across most professions.

For whatever reasons, a substantial number of Harvard graduate students and Ph.D.'s express interest in exploring nonacademic career alternatives and seeking nonacademic jobs. Although faculty acceptance of nonacademic paths is greater now than a decade ago, these potential career changers often do not receive much support or assistance from their departments or faculty advisers, whose experience and expertise lie in academic careers. By the same token, the students themselves are usually ill-equipped to navigate this process on their own, having focused for years on the well-defined but somewhat insular academic world. This guide is for any graduate student or Ph.D. who wants to explore alternatives to a traditional academic career or to actively seek nonacademic jobs. It can be used either as a primary resource or as a supplement to individual career counseling.

Some Underlying Assumptions

First, *exploring alternatives can be liberating, empowering, and fun*. This process may even confirm your original choice of an academic career, but whatever the outcome, you will be better off for your exploration. Viewing the entire process as an adventure in getting to know yourself better, as well as an opportunity to learn what is outside the ivory tower, will help get you started *and* keep you going.

Second, *career exploration and job searches are essentially matchmaking processes*, where both you and the employer are looking for a good "fit." It is important to define "fit" in terms of work that engages, energizes, and fulfills you. Keeping this in mind empowers you to make decisions on your own behalf; you might otherwise feel compelled to take any reasonable job offer.

At the same time, remember that most jobs and careers involve *tradeoffs* (e.g., more money for less autonomy). Thus, you will need to continually question and redefine the line between not compromising on fundamental job requirements and setting unrealistic and inflexible goals.

Third, *be open to the role of serendipity and unpredictability in career development*. Remember that few decisions are irreversible, so that you needn't be paralyzed by a fear of making the "wrong" choice. It is also true, however, that *a systematic exploration and job search almost always pays off*—it increases the probability of finding a good match, being open to the unexpected, and making a wise decision. All of this requires time, energy, focus, patience, persistence, and a belief in yourself.

Plan of the Book

This guide aims to teach a *process* of career exploration and job search that will serve you throughout your career. Although this is necessarily a linear presentation, bear in mind that the process is mostly circular, with each stage affecting most of the others.

There are three major phases or aspects to this process, which are reflected in the structure of the book: self-assessment, exploration of career alternatives, and the job search.

Chapter 1 describes the process of self-assessment and offers some exercises to get you started.

Chapter 2 describes the process of exploring various careers, while Chapter 3 provides an overview of substantive fields of particular appeal to graduate students and Ph.D.'s, categorized in terms of career areas, as well as organizational functions and skills. A sampling of career changes made by GSAS alumni gives a more concrete idea of the range of possible careers and career paths.

Chapter 4 shows you how to strengthen your case as a graduate student or Ph.D. seeking work in fields for which you were not specifically trained. It presents ways to substantively strengthen your credentials, as well as ways to best present yourself through your resume and cover letters.

Launching the job search and getting the job are discussed in Chapter 5—the process and logistics of generating job targets, getting and conducting interviews, and responding to the offer. A section on dual-career strategies concludes the chapter.

Chapter 6 considers special concerns of foreign graduate students who wish to find jobs in the U.S. for their practical training year or beyond.

Finally, Chapter 7 discusses the process of job negotiation and concludes with a few tips on making the transition to a new job in a nonacademic environment.

---

1. *Prospects for Faculty in the Arts and Sciences: A Study of Factors Affecting Demand and Supply 1987 to 2012*, coauthored by William G. Bowen and Julie Ann Sosa, predicted that demand would exceed supply for Ph.D.'s, particularly in the Humanities and Social Sciences beginning in the mid-1990s. They identified several demographic factors accounting for the predicted demand for Ph.D.'s: rising numbers of undergraduates (immigrants and children of baby boomers), large-scale retirements of faculty granted tenure in the 1960s expansion period, and a decline in the number of Ph.D.'s granted. The study has been criticized for not taking into account probable increases in the supply of Ph.D.'s, both from higher graduate student enrollments and the existing pool of underemployed Ph.D.'s, as well as decreases in demand from rising student/faculty ratios. Meanwhile, the recession of the early 1990s has substantially curtailed even "normal" academic hiring, especially at state colleges and universities. In most fields the academic job market has been unusually soft for the past two years, with fewer advertised jobs and many of those withdrawn when funding did not materialize. In addition, the diversion of federal funds away from basic research in the sciences resulting from budget constraints and the end of the Cold War has further depressed the academic market for certain science disciplines.

Chapter 1

ಹಿ

Know Thyself!

Self-Assessment

To know yourself is, of course, the task of a lifetime, but it is also an essential first step in exploring alternative careers. Self-assessment includes asking yourself: what are my most important values, goals, interests, and skills, particularly as they relate to work—the career field, the job function, the environment and people, and the lifestyle implications? This self-knowledge will not only help you to focus your exploration and job search and to narrow options, but it will also substantially increase your chances of getting a job. Employers find it hard to resist candidates who convey an understanding of and conviction about the match between themselves and the job. And once you're in the job, you'll perform with better results *and* greater pleasure.

This chapter focuses on the internal dimension: *Who am I at this point in my life?* and *What does that suggest about my choice of work and careers?* The next two chapters will consider the external dimension: *How do I discover what is out there that matches me?* The premise here is that people are happiest when their work is a vocation, that is, when they are doing jobs or tasks that give them a sense of purpose and meaning, and which they would choose to do even if they did not get paid. This work may be paid or unpaid and of high or low status; it may take many forms and may well change over the course of a life and career. You may need to make compromises along the way for legitimate reasons; the trick is to hold the goal firmly in sight while compromising. Because we spend so much time in gainful employment, we might as well aim for paying jobs that fulfill us, realizing at the same time that fulfilling work is generally a necessary but not sufficient condition for a fulfilling life.

You may find the diagram below helpful for thinking about the process of self-assessment. Typically, in this process you try to ascertain your *values and goals, interests and passions, and skills and capacities* (especially those you most enjoy using or would like to develop). You then consider how they affect your preferences about various aspects of work. These include: (1) the *work environment,* i.e., the physical characteristics of the workplace, organization size, culture, the people—both clients and colleagues (their characteristics and the types of relationships you have with them); (2) the *conditions and lifestyle implications* of the work, e.g., stability, income and benefits, prestige, time commitments, flexibility; (3) the *tasks and functions* you will perform and the associated work style; and (4) the *substantive* content—the organizational mission or product/service, the field, or profession. Note that your

WORK ENVIRONMENT
People: Colleagues & clients
Sociological/Organizational:
Size, structure
Physical: Work space, comfort,
safety, aesthetics

LIFESTYLE IMPLICA-TIONS OF THE WORK
Income, benefits, prestige, security, travel, balance with family and other activities, autonomy, flexibility, pressure, hours, commute

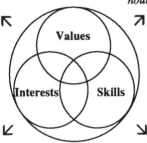

Values

Interests   Skills

FIELD
Substance, content, mission, or product/service of organization

JOB TASKS/SKILLS
Work style, function in organization or endeavor (e.g., marketing, sales, human resources, production/ operations, management, R&D)

skills primarily affect your choice of tasks; interests, primarily your choice of substantive area and the organization's purpose, product, or service; and values, your preferences regarding work environment and lifestyle implications, as well as organizational mission.

Some of you may have a clear sense of your values, interests, and skills and even of purpose or vocation, but those of you who "glided" from college to graduate school may not have needed to pay them much attention. Now is the time to begin clarifying your talents, passions, motivations, goals, and values. It will help to talk to your friends, spend some time by yourself thinking, and even notice your daydreams and fantasies. Homer Hagedorn, a consultant with Arthur D. Little, Inc. whose Ph.D. is in history, recalls "with the wisdom of hindsight" the many clues he ignored as a graduate student that academia was not for him: the "torture" of graduate school, the choice of a dissertation topic on management consulting, the visceral negative reaction he had to the atmosphere at the annual American Historical Association meeting. Pay attention to your intuitive responses, he urges.[1]

To Finish or Not to Finish

Before engaging in a structured self-assessment process, you may need to address the issue of whether or not to finish your Ph.D. This is a highly personal and individual decision and can be a very complex and difficult one, so it is important to remember that you are not alone. Here are a few guidelines for grappling with the issue.

• *Try to separate the "shoulds" from your own true voice.* The "shoulds" come from a variety of sources, including parents and other family members, significant others, professors, mentors, peers, and people who advise you on the new career. You may in the end decide to heed some of the "shoulds," but make this a conscious choice, giving full weight to the "I want" as well.

• *Think not only about the substantive reasons for finishing or not, but also about how you will feel about "quitting."* For some, it may be a source of lasting regret or a psychological burden; for others, it may be a long-overdue declaration of independence. Try to imagine how you will

1. From a panel on Consulting Careers, held at OCS, March 18, 1992.

feel looking back at this decision ten or twenty years from now. Note, however, that you will probably rationalize your choice, whatever it is; most GSAS alumni who have shared their experiences express no regrets about their choice, whether they finished or not (the majority in the Career Advisory Service have finished). If you decide not to finish, think about how you will explain that decision to a potential employer, your spouse, your children, etc.

• *Gather as much information as possible about the practical consequences of either choice for a career in the field(s) you are considering.* Ask people in the field for their advice. Would they make a different decision in hindsight? Does a Ph.D. benefit you more down the line than at the beginning? Is it a negative? Even while you consider the practical consequences, don't lose sight of the *less* practical and tangible ones (as noted above).

• *How close you are to finishing is often a key factor, so also gather practical information about that process.* Find out, for instance, whether it can be accelerated or stretched out to accommodate part-time training or work. Consensus exists on one point: if you know you are leaving academia but want to get the degree, settle for an *acceptable* dissertation rather than a stellar one, and finish it *quickly.*

• *Talk with people whose judgment and discretion you trust.* You might make a list of pros and cons and then balance that analytical approach with listening to your "gut reactions." As you come to a decision (which may take a long time), live with it for a while longer to see how it feels. If possible, take actions that preserve your options rather than close them off, such as requesting a leave of absence instead of withdrawing.

Exercises[2]

The following exercises will help you get started; choose the ones that appeal to you most or seem most valuable, but try to do at least one each for values, skills, and interests. Several exercises give information about all of these, as well as more general clues about "vocation." It is

2. Credit for #2 goes to Richard Bolles, *What Color Is Your Parachute,* for #5 to Barbara Sher, *Wishcraft* , #8 to Kurt Leland (personal communication with the author), and parts of others to Marcia Perkins-Reed, *When 9 to 5 Isn't Enough.* Credit for the values and skills lists is separately noted.

useful to write down your answers so that you can look back on them. If
you are inclined to experiment, try drawing or symbolizing your responses in some way.

1. Make a two-column list of everything you can think of that you like
    and dislike about an academic career, and then assign priorities. What
    do you learn about your values, interests, and skills as they affect the
    work and workplace?

2. Think back over the experiences you have had in your life—in the
    areas of work, leisure, or learning—and pick three to ten that have the
    following characteristics:

    (a) you were the chief, or a significant, actor; (b) YOU—not
    the world or significant others—regard it as a success: you achieved,
    did, or created something with concrete results, or acted to solve a
    problem, or gave something of yourself that you are proud of and
    pleased by; and (c) you truly enjoyed yourself in the process.

    List each of them, write why you consider it a success, and write
    a paragraph or two detailing the experience, step by step. Extract
    from these stories the values and interests they reveal about you and
    the skills you used. In other words, what do they reveal about what
    you like to do and do well? (See the skills list at the end of the chapter
    for help in identifying skills.) This exercise works well if you also tell
    your stories aloud to one or two friends and ask them to reflect back
    to you the skills, qualities, and values they perceive.

3. Think about interest indicators: What do you do in your spare time?
    If you were given $500 to spend in a bookstore, what would you spend
    it on? Is there a cause you feel passionately about?

4. What do you daydream or fantasize about? Are there patterns in these
    daydreams or even your dreams that are indications of your vocation?
    Do you visualize yourself in certain work situations or environments?
    If you have a role model, what about his or her work is relevant to you?

5. If you could live five (or whatever number you want) lives *simulta-
    neously*, and explore a different talent, interest, or lifestyle in each,
    what would you be in each of them? Let your imagination go wild and
    silence the practical "critic."

6. Where do you see yourself in two years? five years? ten years? Include both your personal and professional life. Try visualizing in great detail a day or week in your life at a set time from now, e.g., five years.

7. Imagine you are writing your epitaph or obituary. What would you like to be remembered for? What would you do if you knew you could not fail? What would you do if you had only a year to live and were guaranteed success?

8. Make a two-column list of "characteristics any job I take *must* have" and "characteristics it *must not* have." This list will be very preliminary, and you will constantly revise it throughout this process and beyond. But making the list will help you capsulize your knowledge to date and keep you focused on your central values and requirements. It can also keep you from compromising on essential things when you get a job offer.

9. Look through the following list of work-related values, changing the terminology or concepts as they apply to you, and adding any more general life values that you want to consider. Then rate the degree of importance that you would assign to each for yourself, using this scale:

> 1 = Not important at all
> 2 = Somewhat, but not very important
> 3 = Reasonably important
> 4 = Very important in my choice of career

Take your ten top values (presumably all 4's) and do the priority-setting exercise using the grids on p. 13. (For a quicker, less rigorous version, simply number the ten most important values in order of priority.)

Work-Related Values[3]

___ *Social service*: Do something to contribute to the betterment of my community, country, society, and/or the world.

___ *Service*: Be involved in helping other people in a direct way, either individually or in small groups.

3. Adapted from various lists common in the literature.

___ *People contact*: Have a lot of day-to-day contact with people—either clients or the public and/or have close working relationships with a group; working collaboratively.

___ *Work alone*: Do projects by myself, without any significant amount of contact with others.

___ *Friendships*: Develop close personal friendships with people as a result of my work activities or have work that permits time for close personal friendships outside of work.

___ *Competition*: Engage in activities that pit my abilities against others where there are clear win-and-lose outcomes.

___ *Job pressure/Fast pace*: Work in situations with high pressure to perform well and/or under time constraints; fast-paced environment.

___ *Power/Authority*: Have the power to decide courses of action, policies, etc. and/or to control the work activities or affect the destinies of other people.

___ *Influence*: Be in a position to change attitudes or opinions of other people.

___ *Knowledge*: Engage myself in the pursuit of knowledge, truth, and understanding or work on the frontiers of knowledge, e.g., in basic research or cutting-edge technology.

___ *Expertise/Competence*: Being a pro, an authority, exercising special competence or talents in a field, with or without recognition.

___ *Creativity*: Create new ideas, programs, organizations, forms of artistic expression, or anything else not following a previously developed format. (Specify type of creativity.)

___ *Aesthetics*: Be involved in studying or contributing to truth, beauty, culture.

___ *Change and Variety:* Have work responsibilities that frequently change in content and setting; avoidance of routine.

___ *Job stability and/or security:* Have a predictable work routine over a long period and/or be assured of keeping my job and a reasonable salary.

___ *Recognition/Prestige/Status:* Be recognized for the quality of my work in some visible or public way; be accorded respect for my work by friends, family, and/or community.

___ *Challenging problems:* Have challenging and significant problems to solve.

___ *Career advancement:* Have the opportunity to work hard and make rapid career advancement.

___ *Physical challenge:* Have a job that makes physical demands that I would find rewarding.

___ *Excitement/Adventure:* Experience a high degree of (or frequent) excitement in course of my work; have work duties that involve frequent risk taking.

___ *Wealth or Profit:* Have a strong likelihood of accumulating large amounts of money or other material gain.

___ *Independence:* Be able to work/think/act largely in accordance with my own priorities.

___ *Moral fulfillment:* Feel that my work contributes significantly to, and/or is in accordance with, a set of moral standards important to me.

___ *Location:* Find a place to live that is conducive to my lifestyle and affords me the opportunity to do the things I enjoy most or provides a community where I can get involved.

___ *Self-Realization/Enjoyment:* Do work that allows realizing the full potential of my talents and/or gives high personal satisfaction and enjoyment.

List here the values (titles only) receiving a rating of "4" (do not prioritize). Leave the "score" column blank at this point.

SCORE	VALUES
_____	1.
_____	2.
_____	3.
_____	4.
_____	5.
_____	6.
_____	7.
_____	8.
_____	9.
_____	10.

Now compare each value, in turn, with each of the others, circling on the grid below the number of the most important value in each comparison. So, for example, to compare value #1 with the others, move from left to right across the first double row.

1/2	1/3	1/4	1/5	1/6	1/7	1/8	1/9	1/10
	2/3	2/4	2/5	2/6	2/7	2/8	2/9	2/10
		3/4	3/5	3/6	3/7	3/8	3/9	3/10
			4/5	4/6	4/7	4/8	4/9	4/10
				5/6	5/7	5/8	5/9	5/10
					6/7	6/8	6/9	6/10
						7/8	7/9	7/10
							8/9	8/10
								9/10

FINAL PRIORITIZED LISTING

VALUES

1. _____
2. _____
3. _____
4. _____
5. _____
6. _____
7. _____
8. _____
9. _____
10. _____

To find your scores, count the number of "1's" circled, the number of "2's," and so on. This will give you the score for each value, which can be placed in the "score" column above. If two numbers have the same score, break the tie by looking at the grid to see how you compared those two numbers. On the basis of these scores, construct a final list of values prioritized in this way.

Beyond the foregoing exercises, think specifically and broadly about the skills you have developed as a student and teacher/researcher. Go beyond the obvious ones—the analytical, research, investigative, communication, teaching, and discipline-related skills (such as computer, lab, languages, arts, and substantive expertise). Include abilities such as the following, which were "brainstormed" by a group of graduate students considering nonacademic careers: learning quickly; synthesizing information; problem solving; dealing with complexity, ambiguity, and uncertainty; leadership/managerial or administrative/planning/budgeting skills; people skills, including the ability to motivate and counsel students, persuasion, tact, and political savvy; evaluation skills; and personal qualities such as self-motivation, self-discipline, initiative, creativity, focus, meticulousness, stamina, independence, and humor.

Think also in terms of underlying or "tacit" skills.[4] To take one example, a host of implicit capacities undergirds teaching: translating and explaining difficult concepts; defining objectives of a course or lecture; formulating a strategy for achieving the objectives; locating, retrieving, and evaluating potential materials; abstracting, summarizing, and organizing those materials into an effective written and/or oral presentation; time management; "psyching out," motivating, and nurturing students; evaluating performance; collaborating and cooperating.

The bottom line is that you want to think in terms of *transferable skills*—i.e., skills that can be generalized and hence are valuable in many jobs and settings. In her new position as a fundraiser for an Ivy League university, Donna Consolini has discovered the transferability of the skills she gained as a graduate student: "Running a business meeting in Cincinnati is not unlike teaching a discussion section; writing reports and letters is easy because I like to write; researching financial and business information reminds me of how I felt beginning to research in a foreign language when I started in German years ago."[5]

Similarly, Michael Yogg, Ph.D., now Senior Vice-President at State Street Research, found his graduate training in history to be highly relevant to his new career:

4. Bennett, *Playing Hardball With Soft Skills*, Chapter 3.
5. Donna Consolini, letter to the author, April 10, 1992.

Four qualities distinguish every successful investment professional: intellectual honesty, diligence, intelligence, and creativity. Among these honesty is paramount. Scholarly training
develops all of these traits; it is the best way, to my mind, of
developing a passion for intellectual honesty.... [E]ncountering
evidence in the world of scholarship and facing the facts of the
investment world are very similar intellectual and emotional
experiences. The games are different but the rules are the same.
Like the scholar, the investor seeks to discover value that others
have missed, either by unearthing new facts or by rethinking old
scenarios.[6]

And Karen Lech, whose technical expertise in molecular biology was a
prerequisite for being hired as a patent agent at the Boston law firm Fish
& Richardson, stresses the additional importance of the writing and
teaching skills she developed in graduate school. She constantly applies
these to writing patent applications and educating inventors and patent
examiners.

A final word on skills: do not sell yourself short in this area. As
one GSAS student put it, "Harvard is the academic equivalent of Parris
Island. The fact that Harvard Boot Camp demoralizes you does not mean
you are not capable."[7]

You may want to use the following skills list to help you identify
and prioritize your skills. Circle all the skills that you have used in past
and present jobs or hobbies, in school or extracurricular activities, or at
home. Look for patterns, especially whether these skills tend to relate to
people, data, or things. Then select the ones you most enjoy using or want
to develop further, and list your top five to ten in order of importance.

6. The Regents of the University of the State of New York, *Teaching and Beyond: Nonacademic Career Programs for Ph.D.'s* (Regents of the University of the State of New York, New York, NY, 1984), 21-22.
7. Rob Scheinerman, letter to the author, June 5, 1992.

Skills [8]

Administering
>   a department of people, programs
>   a specific activity

Analyzing and Classifying
>   quantitative, statistical, physical, and/or scientific data
>   human/social situations
>   classifying information into categories or people into programs

Anticipating
>   staying one step ahead of public moods
>   able to sense what will be fashionable in consumer goods
>   expecting a problem before it develops, seeing the first signs

Auditing/Accounting
>   assessing the financial status of an organization

Calculating and/or Risk Management
>   performing mathematical computations
>   assessing risks of a contemplated activity

Collaborating/Teamwork
>   attaining objectives through group/team/committee processes

Conceptualizing/Abstracting
>   parts of a system into a whole
>   ideas from surface events
>   new spacial relationships
>   non-observable physical phenomena
>   concepts, interpretations

Constructing and/or Repairing
>   mechanical apparatus, electronic equipment
>   physical objects, furniture, etc.
>   houses/buildings

8. Adapted from a list from Radcliffe Career Services, based on Howard Figler's *The Complete Job Search Handbook*, with input from various standard sources, which are listed in the Bibliography.

Coordinating (see also organizing)
>   numerous events involving different people
>   great quantities of information
>   activities in different physical locations
>   events in time sequence

Counseling/Advising/Group Facilitating
>   helping or advising people individually, in groups, in various organi-
>   zations with personal/emotional concerns, life development con-
>   cerns (career, finances, education), and/or family matters

Creating
>   artistically (visual arts, performing arts, crafts, music, writing)
>   new ideas for an organization
>   new ways of solving mechanical problems
>   ways of inventing new equipment, processes, materials

Dealing with Pressure
>   risks toward self, physical or otherwise, and/or risks toward others
>   time pressure, deadlines
>   complaints, abuse from others

Dealing with Unknowns
>   making decisions based on severely limited information
>   making hypotheses about virtually unknown phenomena

Decision Making
>   about the use of money
>   about alternative courses of action
>   involving physical safety of others

Delegating
>   distributing tasks to others; giving responsibility to others

Designing and/or Drawing
>   layouts for printed media, public displays, or other commercial
>   purposes
>   advertisements
>   physical interiors of rooms
>   buildings of all kinds
>   clothing
>   exhibits
>   commercial drawing/photography

Developing Mathematical/Statistical Models
    for scientific, economic, other behavioral phenomena

Displaying
    ideas in artistic form
    products in store windows
    equipment, mechanical devices

Editing/Revising
    newspaper, magazine pieces
    book and other manuscripts

Enduring/Persisting
    long hours of work, physical danger or hardship, periods of solitude,
        or "difficult" people
    failures/obstacles

Evaluating/Appraising/Comparing
    evaluating the performance of individuals
    evaluating programs or services in terms of objectives
    judging the value of property
    judging similarity or divergence of data, people, or things from
        obvious standards

Fundraising/Soliciting—for variety of causes
    on person-to-person basis or from large foundations and organizations
    through advertising or sale of products or fundraising events
    for political candidates

Handling Complaints
    from customers, stockholders, citizens, clients

Handling Detail or Precision Work
    doing numerous small tasks efficiently; attending to small details
    working on physical materials or with data with little margin for error
    working with small motor dexterity

Initiating
    new ideas, approaches, ways of doing things
    new projects
    contacts with people, strangers

Interpreting/Translating
　other languages, cultures
　obscure phrases or passages
　meanings associated with statistical data
　highly technical, abstract, sophisticated concepts/language to simpler
　　terms

Interviewing/Questioning
　evaluating applicants to an organization
　obtaining information from others
　obtaining evidence in legal situations
　asking creative questions in fluid situations

Investigating/Finding
　seeking hard-to-find or withheld information
　seeking underlying causes for a problem
　finding information in obscure, remote, or varied sources
　locating potentially helpful people

Listening
　to one person or extended conversations between others in order to
　　help
　to recording devices or other monotonous listening situations

Managing
　being responsible for the work of others
　organizing, coordinating, and developing human, informational, and
　　material resources to effect greater productivity or otherwise meet
　　the objectives of an organization or department
　guiding the activities of a team (athletic or otherwise)

Meeting the Public
　being a public representative of an agency or organization
　being a tour guide, park ranger
　selling products in a public place
　dealing with the public in a service capacity
　acquiring information (survey taker)

Motivating or Leading
　persuading others to help or follow you
　motivating others for peak physical or psychological performances

Moving with Dexterity, Speed, Grace
>   can involve large and/or small muscle coordination
>   athletic ability

Negotiating/Mediating
>   negotiating contracts or other deals
>   mediating between individuals or groups in conflict
>   facilitating positive interaction of members of a group

Observing and Inspecting
>   physical phenomena with great accuracy
>   behavior of human beings or social/historical changes
>   inspecting physical objects to meet standards, or observing people to
>   determine criteria or detect information

Organizing
>   bringing people together for certain ends, creating new groupings for
>   a common purpose
>   gathering information and arranging it in clear, interpretable form
>   arranging political activity, rousing the public to action
>   organizing time efficiently

Performing and/or Entertaining
>   performing in dramatic or musical or artistic productions
>   entertaining people with stories, actions, jokes in small informal
>   settings or in front of an audience
>   news anchor, talk show host
>   social entertaining

Planning
>   anticipating future needs of a company/organization
>   scheduling a sequence of events or itinerary

Politicking
>   generating support for one's ideas within an organization or from the
>   public
>   influencing policy within an organization/firm
>   generating financial support from another agency/organization

Programming
>   computers
>   developing and arranging a sequence of events

Reading
>   large amounts of material quickly
>   written materials with great care
>   numbers or symbols

Record Keeping/Collating
>   orderly keeping of numerical data or financial records
>   creating and maintaining files (computer, paper)

Rehabilitating
>   helping people to resume use of physical limbs
>   working with patients through media such as art and music

Remembering
>   large quantities of information for immediate recall
>   names, faces, places, etc.
>   long sequences of events or instructions

Researching and Compiling
>   extracting information from libraries, people, physical data
>   locating information in obscure, remote, or varied sources
>   gathering statistical data or facts on a given topic
>   critically investigating or experimenting with aim of revising accepted
>   conclusions in light of newly discovered facts

Selling/Persuading/Influencing
>   selling ideas to others in person or in writing or images
>   selling products to individual households or companies
>   selling government policies to the public
>   persuading others to help or follow you, or see your point of view

Speaking
>   speaking publicly to an audience or individually to many people
>   speaking on media

Supervising/Monitoring
>   directly overseeing the work of others in various settings, e.g., white-
>   collar workers, laborers
>   following the progress of another person or of equipment
>   overseeing a physical plant, building, etc.

Synthesizing
>   combining items of information into a coherent whole

Teaching and/or Coaching
>   teaching in the school or college classroom
>   tutoring individuals in certain subjects
>   training individuals to perform certain tasks
>   guiding the activities of an athletic team

Toleration
>   of misbehavior or mistakes of people you are responsible for
>   of lack of support or understanding of the work you are doing
>   of anonymity or lack of recognition for your work

Troubleshooting/Problem Solving
>   finding sources of difficulty in human relations or physical systems
>   conceiving solutions to problems

Using Instruments
>   assembling technical apparatus
>   using scientific, medical, or technical instruments
>   obtaining accurate scientific measurements

Working Outdoors
>   involvement with the land and its resources, and/or animal and plant
>   life
>   testing oneself against physical challenges
>   collecting scientific data

Writing (see also editing)
>   copy writing for sales/advertising   proposal/grant writing
>   technical and scientific writing   expository writing, essays
>   creative writing, prose, poetry   popular writing/journalism
>   report/memo writing, correspondence

    The above exercises represent a fraction of the possibilities for self-assessment, some of which are listed in the Bibliography. In addition, you can take vocational interest tests such as the Strong Interest Inventory and the Jackson Vocational Interest Survey, which are offered at the Office of Career Services (OCS). These tests suggest career fields that fit your expressed interests, work styles and roles, and other preferences, based on profiles of people already in those careers.[9]

9. The Myers-Briggs Trait Inventory has been popular as an indicator of work predilections and styles and can be taken at Radcliffe Career Services, among other places.

As you look back over your responses to the exercises you have chosen, try to find common themes. List your values, interests, and skills in order of priority. Also list the top few characteristics of the work environment, conditions, people, and tasks or work style. As you go on to the next phase of the process, be prepared to alter your priorities as you discover more about what particular careers and jobs are like. And go back to the self-assessment process from time to time, to discover and respond to how you have changed in the meantime.

Chapter 2

෨

Exploring Alternative Careers: The Process

Having done some serious self-assessment, you are ready to explore what alternatives outside academia make sense for you. This involves narrowing your focus and clarifying the match between your needs and particular careers and jobs. (Continue to bear in mind that the process is circular and that each stage allows refinement of the others.) This is essentially a research project, and you are already an expert at research; indeed, you may have to fight the temptation to linger too long in this familiar territory. Your sources are library materials and, *primarily*, people in jobs.

Initial Brainstorming

You might begin your exploration by brainstorming possible careers in a structured fashion. This can be done in various complementary ways: with a career counselor, alone with paper and pencil following the model provided below, or with friends and acquaintances.

Involving at least one other person adds the benefit of multiple perspectives and "group" synergy. For example, you could tell a friend or group of friends your top three to five values, interests, and skills and ask for any and all suggestions on careers combining them. At this stage do not interrupt the creative process with reasons why the suggestions are impractical. Later on you can discuss obstacles and objections to your heart's content, so long as you are committed to looking for ways to overcome them, preferably with some additional brainstorming help from your friends.[1]

To give you an idea of what might emerge from the process, consider the following examples from a workshop brainstorming session. The first describes John (not his real name), a new Ph.D. in the physical sciences:

Values	Interests	Skills
enjoyment	outdoors/nature/environment	imagining/creating
free time	photography/visual media	counseling/tutoring
self-realization	travel/foreign cultures	managing/mediating
independence	history	investigating/interpreting

Possible work/careers:

- teacher, administrator for Outward Bound or similar programs combining teaching with environmental context
- freelance nature and/or cultural photographer, e.g., for National Geographic
- environmental policy work, especially international, e.g., for the United Nations or Institute for Applied Social Science Analysis
- park ranger
- documentary maker
- manager of an international cultural and/or educational exchange program
- science writer, editor [writing was a skill, but not among the top]
- creator/promoter/coordinator/guide for exotic travel packages or international conferences

1. Madeleine Pelner Cosman, in *Kissing the Dragon*, offers a different and valuable approach (aimed mainly at Humanities Ph.D.'s), which can be adapted to a brainstorming session. Focusing on two or three marketable skills ingeniously packaged with your academic expertise, ask yourself how you can make them work together in unusual settings, such as "unlikely" colleges and universities, educational sections of cultural institutions, or in enterprising projects for business or industry.

- educator, manager of a science museum
- public education specialist for environmental interest group
- teacher at all levels in various settings (science, outdoors-related, photography)
- financial analyst for scientific enterprises [based more on academic field than on listed values, interests, and skills]
- technical and/or environmental consultant

"Jane," a graduate student in the humanities, generated the following:

Values	Interests	Skills
competence	teaching/pedagogy	writing
aesthetics	theater/literature	reading
creativity	public relations	observation
independence/time flexibility		entertaining
		endurance

Possible work/careers:

- theater critic
- documentary maker, e.g., on different art forms or education
- playwright
- public relations for arts organizations, film festivals, international artistic exchanges [takes into account her international background]
- stand-up comic [based on group response to personality, as well as skills]
- teacher in various settings (schools, colleges, workshops, international tours)
- editor, publisher in fields of interest
- founder, director of a theater arts program or school

You may prefer to start with the more analytic brainstorming exercise on the next page, which can be done alone. Either form of brainstorming will get you started in the exploration process and may be re-employed in a modified form at any point along the way, to expand possibilities even as you narrow your focus.

BRAINSTORMING

This is an example of one person's brainstorming exercise. Pick your top five skills, interests, and values and then intersect each set with each other.

Data on J. Miller

SKILLS:
writing/researching
designing
teaching
sketching/photography

INTERESTS:
old houses
furniture
energy policy

VALUES:
working independently
moving around on the job
using hands

MAIN FOCUS ON INTEREST: *"OLD HOUSES"*

MY SKILLS...   *MAYBE I COULD...*

WRITING/RESEARCHING
DESIGNING

1. Consult to homeowners who want to restore authentically
2. Make doll house models
3. Make museum exhibits

1. Write for local paper on historic houses
2. Work for a national historic sites organization
3. Research histories of houses for owners

TEACHING
1. Lead walking tours of historic areas
2. Give course on architectural history of an area

SKETCHING/PHOTOGRAPHY
1. Do drafting for architectural firm
2. Sketch or photograph homes for notepaper or cards

MAIN FOCUS ON SKILL: *"WRITING/RESEARCHING"*

MY INTERESTS...   *MAYBE I COULD...*

OLD HOUSES

1. Write for local paper on historic houses
2. Work for a national historic sites organization
3. Research histories of houses for owners

FURNITURE
1. Research period furniture for a museum
2. Write for an antiques publication

ENERGY POLICY
1. Investigate alternative energy sources
2. Write material for public on conservation or solar energy
3. Write reports for environmental and energy consulting group

---

MAIN FOCUS ON VALUE: *"USING HANDS"*

MY INTERESTS...   *MAYBE I COULD...*

OLD HOUSES
1. Make museum exhibits
2. Work on construction site renovating houses
3. Make doll house models

FURNITURE
1. Restore antique furniture
2. Upholster furniture
3. Make miniature furniture for doll houses

ENERGY POLICY
1. Work with solar energy devices
2. Make materials for teaching public about energy alternatives

---

Courtesy of Radcliffe Career Services

Practical Considerations

Before we get into the specifics of the research/exploration process, we need to consider some organizational and logistical matters. At this point you may be experiencing a sense of déjà vu as you remember the lack of structure you faced when you began your dissertation research. The sense of multiple possibilities, combined with little knowledge of what exactly exists "out there" in the way of jobs and careers, can be daunting. Even if you have already focused on a career area, you will need to impose a structure and discipline on the search process.

Set aside a block of time for your exploration and set reasonable goals within a given time frame. (Barbara Sher in *Wishcraft* presents an effective system for goal setting, working backward step by step from the final goal to a task you can accomplish immediately.[2]) You may be able to devote a small amount of time each week over several months, or you may have to concentrate your efforts into a few weeks. It helps to make yourself accountable to someone else for achieving the goals you set—agreeing, for example, to report to a friend that you have done one to two hours of library research and one informational interview each week. (See Chapter 5 for a more rigorous, full-time schedule.)

From the outset, it is crucial to maintain a filing system that works for you and to *keep excellent records*. Consider notebooks, file boxes, accordion files, computer files, calendars, or some combination of these. You may want to catalogue in more than one way, for example, by industry/career field and alphabetically. You'll also probably want some summary sheet detailing your contacts, source of referral, meeting date, and noting phone contact, thank-you and other correspondence sent, and important information, especially things to follow up on. Notes detailing your conversations, reactions, and other information about your contacts and their work would be kept separately. This may be tedious, but it will pay off.

Finally, create an attractive draft resume to use as an introduction and for feedback in your networking process. (See Chapter 4 for advice on resumes.)

---

2. Sher, *Wishcraft*, especially Chapter 6.

Sources of Information

Your main sources of information about careers and jobs are library materials and people. Harvard students and alumni can find a wealth of both kinds of sources at the Office of Career Services. Similar resources exist at most colleges and universities and at various private (often nonprofit) career and employment agencies, not to mention public libraries. You will want to use the library and people resources concomitantly.

Library research. For your library research consider the following sources, many of which are available at OCS, Baker Library (Harvard Business School), and Guttman Library (Graduate School of Education), as well as in the community:

1. *Newspapers, journals, periodicals specific to the field.* For example, if you find yourself devouring the *Wall Street Journal, Fortune,* or *Business Week,* not only will you have a good indication of an interest in business as a career, but you'll also gain knowledge of the issues, players, opportunities, and jargon in business, all of which will aid you immeasurably in the job exploration and search process. *Science* devotes an entire issue each spring to science careers. You can also use the daily news to give you ideas of potential growth fields, career niches, or job opportunities; for example, potential business opportunities in Eastern Europe and the former Soviet Union might translate into a job for an area specialist.
2. *Career literature,* some of which is listed in the Bibliography and some of which is available from professional societies, not only from the nonacademic career field, but also from your academic discipline.
3. *Directories,* supplying information on: companies and their personnel, type of work, and products; publications; professional and trade associations; research centers; nonprofit organizations; governmental agencies; schools and colleges/universities; international organizations, etc. The adventurous and unfocused might start with the *Occupational Outlook Handbook* (see the Bibliography).
4. *Corporate annual reports and marketing materials,* available from the companies themselves. OCS has annual reports from many public companies and also *Lotus One Source,* a CD-ROM database with annual reports and journalistic information on 120,000 publicly and privately held companies, updated every quarter.

5. *Novels and journalistic accounts* of particular work or professions or industries (e.g., *Nice Work* by David Lodge, comparing the academic and business worlds, Tom Wolfe's books, Studs Terkel's *Working*).

6. *Job and internship listings* at OCS (especially in the "Ph.D. Nonacademic Jobs" binder) or similar offices, which give specific information about existing jobs and their requirements. Classified ads in both newspapers and specialized publications do the same.

7. *Alumni Career Adviser biographical information*, available at OCS in the Career Advisory Service binders and Class Reports.

Be sure to request assistance from the reference librarian for whatever collection you are using. Again, remember that library research is critical, but don't get mired down in this familiar activity.

Information interviewing. The *best* source of insight into what specific jobs and careers entail, short of actually doing the job yourself, is talking with people working in these fields. This is called *"information (or informational) interviewing."* Don't underestimate the value of the personal, qualitative, and evaluative information it provides. By skillfully questioning people—preferably at their work sites—about the challenges, frustrations, satisfactions, and opportunities of their work and careers, as well as the specifics of their jobs, organizations, and "industries," you can usually determine whether this particular work matches your needs. You might also talk about your values, interests, and skills and later on in the interview ask them whether they think there is a fit or whether they can suggest other possible career niches.

Remember that you need to prepare even for information interviews. Do some library research on the career, the particular company, and the contact *before* you visit or make the phone call, and think about what information you need and the questions that would best elicit it. As you learn more about a profession, you can add more focused questions to your general list. By the way, it helps to get some practice interviewing friends or close colleagues before you tackle the more intimidating or important contacts. If you think there is a potential match, it is appropriate to ask for advice on how to make the transition from academia, to strengthen your credentials, to best present yourself (including your resume), and to find out more about this career or related ones. The importance of building a network cannot be overemphasized; never (well, hardly ever) leave an information interview without at least two more names of people to talk with, requesting permission to use your contact's name as a referral.

At this point, you are mainly gathering information, ruling *in* and ruling *out* options. (The latter is just as valuable as the former.) It is very important that you stick to this agenda and not turn the session into a job interview; people misusing information interviewing in this way have given it a bad name. It also should go without saying that much of the general advice for interviewing presented in Chapter 5 applies to information interviews as well. Present yourself professionally, intelligently, and positively; stay within the time you asked for (usually 20-30 minutes); and express your appreciation for the person's time and help and send a thank-you letter after your interview. At the least, you will leave a positive impression behind; at the most, you may enlist an ally who will offer to help you further when you embark on a job search. You may even be fortunate enough to find a mentor.

How do you find people to talk with about their work? To start, OCS offers a gold mine: the *Career Advisory Service*, a file of alumni who have volunteered to share information and advice about their careers (but not job offers) with Harvard students and alumni. The richest source for your needs is likely to be the subgroup of alumni with M.A.'s and Ph.D.'s, many of whom have changed careers. OCS also has a growing file of 10th- and 25th-Reunion Career Advisers, as well as some through the Harvard Club Alumni network. Otherwise, untether your imagination and ask friends, relatives, fellow alumni, colleagues, professionals whose clients come from all walks of life (e.g., doctors, bankers, realtors, clergy, cosmetologists), other acquaintances and even strangers—such as seatmates on planes—about their work and ask for contacts in the fields of interest to you. You might also consider asking some of these contacts if you could "shadow" them for a day or more to get a more complete picture of what their work is like.

Before going on to other "people" sources of information, it is important to distinguish information interviewing from the more inclusive activity of *network building*. Networking is creating professional contacts and relationships through meetings in business and social gatherings in order to create visibility, gather information about job and other professional opportunities, and receive *and* return professional favors. Having already begun to build your network through your quest for information interviews, use the next stages of your exploration and search to develop it further. You will, of course, continue to expand your network throughout your professional career.

Deborah Daw (Ed.M.) relates an anecdote illustrating effective network building—and several other techniques. Following a stint as an assistant dean at Boston University and then a fellowship at the National Endowment for the Arts, Deborah decided to break into communications consulting. She read a *Globe* article about the Boston Club's project to prod businesses to name more women to their boards of directors. Deborah blithely called Carol Goldberg, one of the women named in the article (but not knowing her identity as the CEO of Stop & Shop), to request an information interview. Asked by her secretary why she needed to see Carol Goldberg, she blurted out: "Because I'm looking to make a career change into business and I'm desperate for a mentor. And tell her I think what she's doing to promote women board members is wonderful!"[3] Apparently Carol was so taken with Deborah's chutzpah that she delegated her director of personnel to meet with her; the result was a freelance position as coordinator of the project, which had been in the hands of the overcommitted committee members. Needless to say, Deborah created an enviable network in the process of collecting, standardizing, and distributing resumes of potential board members to targeted corporations. This came in handy when she became Vice President of Better Communications, Inc., a leading consulting firm specializing in business and technical writing training.

For more detailed information about information interviewing, see the guidelines at the end of the chapter.

Other people sources. Numerous *panel presentations* by GSAS alumni or other Ph.D.'s on nonacademic alternatives and their transitions to them (e.g., consulting, writing, nonprofit and public sector, international, high tech) provide another "people" source of information for Harvard students and alumni; and these panels are usually available on tape. The annual OCS *Business Management Study Group* gives participants a chance to explore business careers and management fields, issues, and cases in a seven-week series of seminar presentations. The seminars are usually led by Harvard Business School faculty or people in business, many of whom themselves have Ph.D.'s in the arts and sciences.

Following the example of many alumni, you might attend the

3. Personal communication with the author.

meetings of *professional and trade associations* in your potential career field, to introduce yourself and ask questions. (Refer to the *Encyclopedia of Associations* and/or ask career advisers for advice.) You do not have to have a formal interview in order to gather a lot of information about a person's work. Indeed, the master interviewer Studs Terkel was overheard chatting with a burglar about his "work," even as he was being held up at his doorstep.

Work or volunteer experience. If you can arrange it, try gaining firsthand information about a career and/or organization by working—for pay or not—as a freelancer, intern, summer or part-time employee, or volunteer. Such *actual work experience* serves multiple functions: it enables you to explore possible careers, refine your self-assessment, strengthen your credentials, and generate a network—and perhaps even employment opportunities. All the people and library sources listed above can serve you in lining up "on-the-job training." Similarly, taking courses related to your career interests can provide you with information about the field, potential contacts, and more knowledge about your skills, interests, and values. (These activities are discussed more fully in Chapter 4.)

Remember to keep excellent notes and records throughout this exploration process. For example, write down your impressions and the information and advice you received immediately after each interview. Spend a few minutes trying to visualize yourself in this job. How does it fit with who you are? How do you feel in the setting? Doing the work? Go back and revise your self-assessment information in light of your increasing knowledge of what exists outside the ivory tower.

A Case in Point: Judy Esterquest

Judy Esterquest provides a good example of creative career exploration. In recounting her transition from academia to business, where she is the Director of Professional Development (worldwide) for Booz Allen and Hamilton Inc., she notes that she always had many interests outside her field of English (specialty: Victorian) literature. To pursue those interests she went about creating opportunities for herself: she audited Harvard Law and Business School courses, asked lots of questions of her friends in those professional schools, read widely outside her field (including specialized publications), and conversed freely with strangers on planes and buses about their work. She also did curriculum development at the Graduate School of Education and the Business School, which served both as a source of information and as a means of strengthening her credentials. As a graduate student consultant on a project to design a new writing program at the "B School," she impressed colleagues with her knowledge of business, experience with teaching and curriculum development, and the fact that she had friends at the school; this led to a part-time job teaching in the new writing program. Thus, when Booz Allen, in searching for a new Director of Professional Development, scanned faculty lists of business schools and randomly picked her name, Judy was well positioned to compete for the job.

INFORMATION INTERVIEWING
A Few Guidelines

Preparation

1. Do your research first.

2. Think carefully about what you hope to learn and the kinds of questions that will elicit that information. Most people prefer to answer questions that require them to reflect on their work; thus, open-ended, evaluative questions are often most effective, especially to begin with. The order and phrasing of your questions will depend on your own style and the flow of the conversation.

   The kinds of information you might want to discuss include:
   - *What the job/work is like*: the challenges, frustrations, rewards encountered; kinds of decisions made, problems solved; how time is spent, etc.
   - *Desirable skills, education, and experience*; required training or preparation
   - *Career paths and advancement*
   - *Lifestyle implications of the work*: e.g., salary/benefits, family policy, travel, pressure, flexibility, security, etc.
   - *Work environment*: physical setting, people (colleagues and clients), organizational structure and culture
   - *Current issues in the "industry"* (beyond what you have read)
   - *Evaluative information on particular companies*
   - *Ways to get more information*: journals, professional organizations, other contacts, possible internship opportunities

3. Start with your least intimidating contacts.

Do

- When writing or calling to request the interview, be clear and direct about the goal of your interview (information, not jobs) and the time commitment (suggest 20-30 minutes). Try to meet with the individual at his or her workplace and convenience, but be prepared to settle graciously for a phone interview, even on the spot if necessary (... so have your questions ready).

• Act professionally, as you would for any interview: call to confirm a day or so ahead, dress appropriately, and arrive a little early so you can experience the work environment and relax before your appointment.

• *Listen* attentively and gear your questions to the flow of conversation, without losing track of the time and your specific goals.

• Jot down any special points, clarify any unfamiliar terms or confusions, and keep track of any referrals or suggestions. Finish writing down what you learned *immediately* after the interview.

• Stay within your time limit, unless the career adviser indicates otherwise. Be sensitive to nonverbal clues that it is time to end the interviews.

• WRITE A THANK-YOU NOTE. The adviser should be thanked for his or her time and thought, even for a phone interview and even if he or she tried to discourage you or does not seem to be in a position to help you in the future. (A handwritten note is fine, but treat it as *professional* correspondence.)

• Even after the thank-you note, keep your contacts informed of your career development progress. Not only do people really appreciate hearing about you, but you maintain your network.

Don't

• Ask for a job—even indirectly.

• Speak with only one or two people and assume their views are representative of the field.

Matters of Judgment

- *Whether to write or call first.* Call first if the person has indicated he or she expects or prefers to be contacted by phone or to confirm information you need to write to him or her. Write first if you think the contact would appreciate having a brief introduction by mail and a sense of what you are exploring. Remember, even when writing, you must follow up with a call. Experiment to see what works best for you.

- *How and when to present a resume.* You should always bring your resume to an information interview, even if you have also included one in your introductory letter. Either way, treat it as an efficient way to give your contact a sense of your background or as something that you seek advice on, rather than as a ploy to get a job.

- *To pay or not to pay* (for the lunch, drink, etc.). A good rule of thumb is "He who invites, offers to pay." So be prepared to offer to pay for both of you, or—as is more likely—to pay your own way, or to graciously accept the adviser's offer to pay.

- *Self-presentation and your own expectations.* Remember first of all to be yourself, but also be sensitive to the impression you make (career advisers have noted in the past the extremes of arrogance and self-deprecation). Make sure that your expectations are realistic: know what you hope to learn about their career field, and don't expect them to offer you a job or to provide you with general career counseling.

- *Going back to ask for job-hunting help.* If you feel you have established rapport with someone, it is reasonable to recontact the person later when you have narrowed your focus and begun a job search. Simply write or call the adviser and remind him or her of your previous contact, explain your current situation and goals, and ask if her or she would mind passing along your resume or letting you know of job leads.

Chapter 3

❧

Nonacademic Careers:
A Mini-tour

This chapter describes some ways to think about the myriad possibilities "out there" as you begin your quest, as well as providing some examples of the various and often unpredictable career shifts made by graduate students and Ph.D.'s. Of course, a brief guide emphasizing the *process* of nonacademic career exploration and change cannot fully satisfy your curiosity and need to know about those possibilities.

Conceptual Frameworks

First, it is useful to distinguish between nonacademic careers directly related to your training, experience, substantive expertise, and skills, and all other careers, for which your training and experience are of no particular benefit and may even be perceived as a liability. The point of this is to alert you to the wide array of possibilities for which you may be already prepared, competitive, and hence easily "marketable." Indeed, a Ph.D. is often required for these jobs. They will be referred to as *quasi-academic* opportunities within a given career field.

Some of you may also find it useful to distinguish jobs/careers by whether or not they are *entrepreneurial*. Creating and running your own business can range from part-time freelance writing and editing, to a solo counseling, consulting, or financial planning practice, to a nonprofit venture like a hospice, to a small for-profit biotech or software company with growth potential. You may regard it as a long-term goal to be achieved after "apprenticeship" as an employee, or a short-term goal that will provide relevant job experience, as in freelance editing or a "once-in-a-lifetime" opportunity *now*. In general, the choice of an entrepreneurial path is motivated less by skills or interests than by personality characteristics and values, such as a strong desire for autonomy and independence (which may also be pursued within organizations) or an overriding need to create a new organization, a new business, or a financial empire.

A third way of organizing your search is to look only for *"growth fields,"* where intelligence, drive, and ambition are more important than specific job-related skills or experience. For example, Michael Yogg, the History Ph.D. quoted on p. 15, entered financial analysis in the late 1970s just before its boom and well before it was flooded with M.B.A.'s.[1] Probable growth fields for the 1990s include the environment, biotechnology, telecommunications and other "high-tech" fields, and health.

Finally, you may want to focus your search utilizing two broad frameworks: the *functional area* and the *career field* (discussed below). The functional area you choose will probably be influenced more by your skills and aptitudes, and the career field more by your values and interests.

Virtually every enterprise and/or organization must perform multiple functions in order to create, distribute, and finance its product(s) or service(s), such as *research and development (R&D), administration (including human resources management), finance, management and strategic planning, production, marketing, and sales.* So, for example, if you want to carry your academic background most directly into either a nonprofit or for-profit enterprise, you would look for positions in R&D or perhaps training and development (in human resources). By contrast, if you know you like management and have wide-ranging interests, you can explore management or administrative careers in any type of organization, realizing, however, that the route to top management positions often begins in one of the "line" positions, such as sales, marketing, or production.

Consulting can be thought of in functional terms and, because it is

1. Rob Scheinerman made this point in a letter to the author, August 5, 1992.

such a popular career option for Ph.D.'s, it deserves special mention. The common denominator of consulting is your ability to diagnose and solve a client's problem(s) and to communicate and help implement those solutions so as to "add value" to the enterprise (above the cost of your services). This applies whether you work for one of the premier management consulting firms or as a solo entrepreneur, whether your clients are for-profit or nonprofit firms, and whether your substantive expertise is organizational development, environmental engineering, education, the arts, or whatever.

Turning now to the second framework, a slightly modified version of the career categories used at OCS yields the following *career fields*:

1. *Business careers* cover a wide range of jobs in the private sector in enterprises of various sizes that produce either goods or services for profit. Because of the sheer number and variety of business careers, it is not surprising to find the majority of A.B.D. and Ph.D. career changers in these private-sector jobs. Adding to the attraction of business careers are numerous *quasi-academic* opportunities: for example, high-tech companies recruit science Ph.D.'s, primarily for research and development jobs, and specialty consulting firms hire Ph.D.'s from the relevant discipline, which is frequently economics or various sciences. (Examples of such firms include those working in the areas of economic analysis, environmental issues, technology assessment, strategic consulting, and organizational development.) As you explore business careers, think in terms both of the *industry* (the analogue to career fields, for example: financial services, communications, retailing, manufacturing) and the *functional area* (for example, R&D, marketing, human resources), and how they fit with your interests, skills, experience, and values.

Examples of GSAS alumni career switches to business include changing from:

- *history* to consulting (note the Winthrop Group described on p. 48), to financial services/investment research, to sales and marketing in own software firm
- *literature* to banking and to advertising
- *foreign language* to international consulting (marketing/public relations) and "cultural" consulting, to international banking
- *anthropology, sociology* to organizational development consulting
- *psychology* to market research

- *Italian* to graphic design firm (entrepreneurial)
- *environmental science* to environmental consulting
- *astrophysics* to space consulting
- *geophysics* to technical consulting/research and to investment banking/venture capital
- *biology, physics* to stock analyst
- *physics, chemistry* to directors of research, technical management, aerospace engineering (e.g., Bell Core, Xerox, IBM, TRW, Lockheed)
- *biochemistry, biology, chemistry* to biotech and pharmaceutical companies, in various functions: research and development, managing, marketing, starting new companies
- *mathematics, computer science, physics* to computer hardware/software design, to programming, to information systems, to recording engineer

2. *Media careers* overlap the other career categories, but their common focus is on the activity and/or skill of communicating information, whether or not the enterprise specializes in communications as do the mass media, publishing companies, and specialty consulting companies. Also included are the occupations of writing, translating, or editing, which can be salaried or freelance. Less obvious examples include jobs in public relations, advertising, corporate communications in the business world, or their functional counterparts in a nonprofit or governmental organization. Numerous *quasi-academic* opportunities exist in the media field, such as university publishing and professional journals, and editing and writing for technical or other specialty publications and/or organizations.

Examples of alumni transitions to media careers include moving from:
- *literature* to technical writing and corporate communications, to advertising, to publishing, to translating, to communications consulting
- *foreign language/area studies* to writing and book packaging, to publishing (university and trade), to international public relations/marketing, to freelance writing
- *history* to journalism and to publishing
- *sociology* to journalism
- *biology, biochemistry, and astronomy* to science writing and editing

3. *Education careers*, while technically within the nonprofit world, should be singled out as the traditional *quasi-academic* route for émigrés

from academia, where academic training is highly relevant and academic options may sometimes be maintained. They include academic administration and student services, secondary school teaching and administration, and many jobs in research centers and foundations. This category also includes a wide range of careers in education for which graduate training in the arts and sciences gives no special advantage, such as preschool and elementary education.

Examples of GSAS alumni educational careers include changing from:

- *most disciplines* to independent secondary school teaching
- *history, English*, etc., to secondary school administration
- *history, Celtic, classics, English*, etc., to university administration —from assistant deans, program and center directors to deans of students, deans of the college, and college presidents
- *English, Romance languages* to professional association administration (American Council on Education, Association of Independent Schools of Massachusetts)
- *American studies* to international educational administration (Institute for International Education)
- *sociology, psychology* to educational testing research (e.g., Educational Testing Services)

4. *Nonprofit careers*, for our purposes, include public service and most cultural and arts jobs. The public service category is immense in itself, including social welfare and health services of all kinds and public interest groups on every conceivable social, cultural, political, and economic issue. In addition to the traditional appeal of the specific values and interests expressed in the organization's mission, M.A.'s and Ph.D.'s may also be attracted to nonprofit careers by the relative ease of entering and advancing in the field and, in some cases, by *quasi-academic* opportunities. Some nonprofit organizations require advanced degrees for certain positions, usually in research and education (for example, research positions at the Guttmacher Institute and in some environmental organizations) or in clinical psychology. Many positions in arts organizations also require graduate training, the most obvious example being curatorial positions in museums.

Examples of GSAS alumni transitions to nonprofit careers include changing from:

- *social policy* to nonprofit consulting and directing an energy conservation organization
- *political science* to head of a community music school
- *psychology* to positions in various mental health organizations
- *art history* to museum curators
- *history* to director of public education at the Union of Concerned Scientists

5. *Public Policy careers* embrace work in government at all levels (local, state, federal, and international), in political campaigns and related organizations, and in non-governmental (usually nonprofit) organizations with a policy focus. *Quasi-academic* positions for specialists with advanced degrees abound at all levels in the public sector, particularly in the federal government. The most common disciplines include economics, public policy, government and other social sciences, area studies, and environmental and health sciences. Academics frequently move in and out of the policy world, spending a few years in government and then returning to academia. Former academics have also made their way down less traditional paths into electoral politics at the state and federal level, political campaigns or party organizations, or to the Foreign Service or Capitol Hill positions.

Examples of alumni transitions to policy and political careers include:

- *economics* to the Federal Reserve Board, Office of Management and Budget, Congressional Budget Office, World Bank, International Monetary Fund, Export-Import Bank
- *social sciences* to the Congressional Research Service, Library of Congress, General Accounting Office, Department of Health and Human Services; to various policy think tanks (RAND, Brookings) and other nonprofit policy organizations (e.g., Chicago Council on Foreign Affairs, Asia Foundation)
- *history, government* to the Foreign Service
- *government, international relations*, etc., to GOP state committee head, to press secretary to the Speaker of the House, to Senate staffs (committee and personal), to state senate
- *archeology* to state archeologist
- *art history* to national and state arts policy organizations (e.g., National Endowment of the Arts, state arts councils)

- *biology, biological chemistry* to Senate and House committee staffs (Science), to the Environmental Protection Agency
- *biophysics* to research at the National Institutes of Health, to a state health department
- *chemistry* to National Science Foundation administrator

The matrix on the following two pages is a variation on this theme, arraying career areas by skills graduate students and Ph.D.'s commonly possess, which are in turn usually related to specific organizational functions. You may want to use examples in the matrix as a starting point. Note the inclusion of a category for international "skills" (including language and foreign area knowledge, as well as experience living in foreign cultures). Many graduate students want to use this kind of expertise, which can be valuable in many corporations or government institutions as they respond to increasing globalization.

Some Profiles in Career Changing

Lending more realism and spice to this mini-tour of nonacademic career fields are the brief stories of a few of your fellow alumni "explorers," who have made successful transitions to nonacademic careers.

Deborah Melone, Radcliffe '61, M.A. in English from Northwestern and A.B.D. in English from George Washington University, is Documentation Manager for Bolt Beranek and Newman Inc., a high-tech company (advanced networking and software technologies). Having interspersed graduate school in English with teaching jobs and child rearing, she finally abandoned the Ph.D. when faced with a grim academic job market, a third child, and the suicide of her dissertation subject, poet John Berryman. She attributes her subsequent career development to networking and tangentially-related previous experience. For example, the fact that she had been an editorial assistant at a publishing company between college and graduate school was critical in getting her back into editing and writing as a production editor at the M.I.T. Press (for very low wages), a job she heard about through the Word Guild (a now defunct collaborative of editors, writers, and graphic artists). Although she had no scientific expertise and edited only non-scientific works at M.I.T., this

CAREER FIELDS BY SKILLS

SKILLS / CAREER FIELD	Research & Analysis	Teaching (Presenting, Inspiring)	Writing/ Communication	Administration & Management
Business & Finance (Including HighTech)	R&D (e.g., bio & high tech), risk analysis (financial inst.), market research, consulting	sales, training & development	corporate communications, communications analysis, advertising & PR	management positions reached from line positions in specific companies
Media	journalism, market research	sales, advertising, radio/TV, journalism	journalism, writing, editing, publishing, advertising & PR	editing, publishing, corporate communications, management
Education	research centers, educational research & evaluation, archival work	teaching (adult ed., secondary, community colleges), freelance lecturing	publishing (specialized, educational), reporting, writing	academic administration (e.g., principal headmaster, college dean)
Nonprofit (Public Service, Arts)	organizations with research efforts, think tanks, research centers, foundations	public education, development, community organizing	PR, newsletter editing for nonprofit or professional publications	administration, management, development (events planning), foundation program mgmt.
Public Policy	Congressional Research Service, analytic division of state or local agency	politics, executive branch position, fundraising, interest groups	speech and report writing for government agencies or interest groups	administration of various public agencies, program management

Problem Solving	People Skills	Technical/ Scientific Skills (incl. Computer Program- ming)	International Expertise (Area Studies, Languages, Intl. Exp.)	Arts & other Creative Skills
consulting, marketing, management	consulting, human resources, sales, management, training & development	info. systems, R&D, CAD, actuarial, consulting on scientific/ tech. matters, software co.'s	cultural consulting, intl. business, country risk analysis in financial institutions	advertising, computer music, technical illustration
investigative reporting, PR, management, specialty consulting	sales/ marketing in publishing, interviewing	specialty publishing, professional journals	specialty publishing, foreign desk of various media	specialty publishing, criticism, dramaturgy, art, illustration, writing, photography
academic administration (e.g., principal, headmaster, college dean), educational consulting	student services (e.g., counseling), academic administration, educational consulting	computers in education (e.g., TERC, EDC), curriculum development	international education, curriculum development, educational tours, conferences	arts education in various settings
management, nonprofit consulting, think tanks	development, management, advocacy	R&D, info. systems, consulting for hospitals & other non- profits, environ. groups	nonprofit orgs. (country or region specific), consulting on intl. health & welfare	community arts orgs., specialty museums, art/drama/ dance/music therapy
most higher- level govt. positions, political/policy research, political consulting	politics (as candidate or staff), fundraising, lobbying	national labs, EPA, NSF, NIH, Census, OTA, intl. scientific agencies	international orgs., federal agencies, Congressional staff, policy think tanks, Peace Corps	administration of arts agencies/ organizations (e.g., NEA, state arts councils)

experience gave her credibility when she applied for a job in the corporate publications department at Bolt Beranek and Newman, which she heard about from a friend in her writing group and which, fortuitously, was managed by a pair of Radcliffe alumnae. She has consciously developed her job there from technical editing, which she found frustrating, to incorporate more writing and initiating of projects, and increasingly, more management. Now she produces proposals and reports, writes the company newsletter and internal corporate and external marketing documents, and manages a staff of writers and secretaries. In addition, she is an "after-hours" poet.

Davis (Dave) Dyer and *Alan Kantrow* were history tutors in Winthrop House and Eliot House, respectively, in the late 1970s. Facing a dismal academic market, Dave and Alan, along with two other friends who were history tutors, vowed to start a company together after getting a few years of business experience. In 1982, the four friends actually got back together and founded the Winthrop Group, a consulting firm specializing in historical research and consulting services. Since then the company has expanded in several directions and now provides research and advice to clients on product liability and environmental litigation, public relations, editorial and transcription services, and "archivist" advice on records management and management information services.

Their individual stories are instructive. For example, *Alan Kantrow* actually turned down an assistant professorship at Barnard and "lucked into" a job, first as a senior research associate and, shortly thereafter, as Associate Editor of the *Harvard Business Review*. He heard about the position through his adviser, who was a friend of the Editor, Ken Andrews (who, as a Ph.D. himself, wanted to try "something different" at the *Review*). About midway through his eight-year tenure at the *Review*, Alan joined the Winthrop Group as a part-time consultant, eventually leaving both positions for a full-time consultancy at the Monitor Corporation. About a year later, he got an "offer he couldn't refuse" to join McKinsey and Company as both the Editor of the *McKinsey Quarterly* and the Director of Practice Communications, which involves helping members of the company worldwide to track, integrate, and reapply the expertise developed in their far-flung projects. He is now Director of Communications for Europe and the Pacific.

Dave Dyer got a job as a research associate at Harvard Business

School, which he heard about in a chance encounter with a friend. He coauthored books with Harvard Business School professors Paul Lawrence and Malcolm Salter, taught management courses at Boston College, and then became Associate Editor of the *Harvard Business Review.* Now, as Managing Director of the Winthrop Group, he spends much of his time managing the staff and marketing their various services.

Richard Rabinowitz, also a History (American Civilization) Ph.D. in the late 1970s, took a very different path, which was shaped by his paradoxically having "both a very strong academic background and interest in American history and a huge disdain for the silliness of academic life." [2] His fascination with theater and children's learning processes, combined with his frustration with graduate school, led him to take a nine-month leave-of-absence job at Old Sturbridge Village. He then returned there as Assistant Director—and later Director—for Museum Education after he had passed his generals. For the next six years he worked full time developing curricular materials, training classroom teachers, and collaborating on the design of the new museum education center at Sturbridge, while working part time on his dissertation. After he was fired (for "political" reasons), Richard flirted with returning to academia, taking a job at Scripps College. It didn't work out and he spent the next four years finishing his dissertation, taking care of his son, and holding a long-distance consulting job as special assistant to the Chairman of the National Endowment for the Humanities on policy and program development.

Then in 1980, having been burned by "numbing and negative experiences with bureaucracies in the museum profession and in government," and because he "liked risk taking and the rewards of being paid for producing something quite concrete," Richard cofounded his own (initially nonprofit) venture, The American History Workshop. Over the past dozen years he has overseen over 300 projects throughout the U.S. and in Israel: planning new museums, history centers, and visitor centers; designing interpretive exhibits and multimedia productions; and consulting on urban and park planning, historical preservation, organizational development, and education issues. Although he sometimes laments the financial insecurity of entrepreneurship in the cultural sector, this path has allowed him to maintain his "fierce independence," devote significant

2. Career Advisory Service material.

time to parenting, and simultaneously pursue a career as an independent scholar and writer of history. (He has produced a scholarly work on 19th-century New England religious experience, a children's book on war and peace, and many reviews and research articles.)

Steve Bennett specialized in Chinese geomancy (in case you didn't know: the "science" of situating residences for the living and tombs for the dead) in Harvard's Regional Studies/Far East Program in the mid-1970s. The gloomy forecasts for academic employment finally drove him to seek his fortune in the quasi-academic fields of publishing, educational research, and public television. During the first few years, his jobs ranged from loading trucks to directing research at a political advertising and consulting firm, to running his own failed entrepreneurial publishing company, to writing histories, annual reports, and brochures for the Peace Corps and other volunteer programs. When this "consultancy" evaporated under Reagan, he returned to Boston and, hearing from a friend about lucrative ghostwriting for physicians and scientists, retooled his resume and contacted the local chapter of the American Medical Writers Association. He accepted the first assignment that came his way, to ghostwrite an article on a highly technical clinical chemistry topic that he knew nothing about. He taught himself enough to write a publishable article, and "over the next three years ... built up a broad base of scientific, technical and medical knowledge, eventually developing a knack for simplifying complex technical issues for lay people. This talent laid the cornerstone for a business that quickly grew from a one-person writing service to a fully-staffed technical publishing and advertising company that produced everything from laboratory training guides and product brochures to software and computer manuals." [3] Since then, Steve has returned to a solo business and has expanded into book packaging (bringing researchers, writers, and publishers together). Meanwhile, he keeps writing his own books (over 35 of them!), many of which are based on his personal experiences, such as *Playing Hardball with Soft Skills* and his latest, the best-selling parenting book, *365 TV-free Activities You Can Do With Your Child*.

Carol Farris took the traditional postdoctoral fellowship path after receiving her Ph.D. in Biological Chemistry from the Division of Medical Sciences, spending two and a half years in a molecular biology lab at the National Institutes of Health (NIH). Toward the end of her fellowship,

3. Bennett, *Playing Hardball With Soft Skills*, xvi.

she realized that she didn't want a standard academic job or a bench career because she enjoyed using her writing, editing, and managerial skills, needed more people contact, and was concerned about the toxicity of the substances she worked with in the lab. In order to ascertain whether she wanted to leave the laboratory environment, to explore administrative and regulatory career alternatives, and to generate job leads, she talked with several senior administrative officials at NIH, as well as scientists in regulatory agencies whom she found through the Harvard "old boy" network" (i.e., alumni she knew in Washington). Her networking, coupled with serendipity, produced two job offers—one at the Food and Drug Administration and the one she took in the new Office of Toxic Substances (OTS) at the Environmental Protection Agency (EPA). The director at OTS just happened to be staffing a new office when she called him about another, less suitable job. Specific technical expertise (which she lacked) was less important than her solid scientific background and communication skills.

What she assumed would be a two-year "revolving door" stint leading to a position in a chemical company has instead resulted in a fourteen-year career at the EPA regulating new and existing toxic chemicals. After a few years of developing the agency's nascent program to implement the Toxic Substances Control Act and later heading the Chemical Inventory Section, Carol took advantage of an opportunity to move out of the "technical ghetto" into the policy area, first as a Special Assistant to the Director and then as a Policy Analyst at OTS. She established her value there sufficiently to have been granted a 23-month maternity leave. In the interim, the OTS Policy staff fell victim to bureaucratic politics, so she has recently returned to a part-time job that is, ironically, closer to her original training—regulating genetically engineered microorganisms, among other things.

Dana Ono, a 1981 Ph.D. in Organismic and Evolutionary Biology, is into his fifth career, if you count his first one as an ichthyologist. By the time he got his doctorate, he realized he was having more fun running a fossil jewelry mail-order business on the side than studying fish, and decided to try to get into the emerging biotech industry. Peddling his writing skills and experience as a technical writer and a staffer for *Highlights for Children* (a children's magazine), he landed a market research position with Damon Biotech, where he moved on to technology evaluation and then was promoted to director of business development. He also met his mentor, a Japanese financier and M.I.T. board member, who taught him how to structure deals between Japanese and American companies, knowledge which he applied in opening Damon's Japanese subsidiary. Later he joined Regis McKenna, a "hot" marketing consulting firm, where he helped small biotech entrepreneurs create companies and launch products and, on the side, cofounded the Mass. Biotechnology Council. Tiring of consulting, he next worked in business development at Integrated Genetics and Enzytech, capitalizing on his strengths in identifying commercial opportunities in new technologies, in putting deals together, and in communicating with both the business and scientific communities. Meanwhile, he put his academic/writer hats back on to edit a recently published book, *The Business of Biotechnology: From the Bench to the Street.* In the fall of 1991, after about a year's planning, he founded Arcturus Pharmaceutical Corporation, a partnership with three M.D.'s who had developed a new dermatology therapy. As a frenetic entrepreneur, Dana has recently passed the baton of running the company to a seasoned pharmaceutical executive. He is currently at work trying to put a new venture together, but has not lost sight of a project to write and illustrate a book for his two young children.

A Final Note

These stories sound much more coherent and compressed than the exploration and job-search process was in reality. Most, if not all, of these career changers went through periods of confusion, lack of focus, anxiety, and discouragement. But they also experienced excitement, exhilaration, and growth.

You may be feeling more overwhelmed than excited at this point—perhaps because you have started out with relatively little focus, or your life is already too full to manage, or you are shy. But do read on. The process detailed in the next chapter can dovetail very well with career exploration. More important, you can creatively adapt the entire process to serve *your* particular needs and timetable. Finally, to gain some perspective, look at it as a lifelong (ad)venture.

Chapter 4

ॐ

Strengthening Your Case

In deciding to pursue a nonacademic career—whether or not you complete the Ph.D.—you are changing careers. This creates significant challenges for you, since employers are generally risk-averse, particularly in a recessionary economy. You need to convince a potential employer both that you are absolutely committed to and confident about this career change and that you are essentially one of them, with the added bonus of a graduate education. Moreover, you must convince an employer that you can "add value" to the enterprise; or, as Arthur D. Little's organizational development consultant Homer Hagedorn puts it, "you can hit the ground running, as well as pay off down the line." In order to persuade a potential employer, you must first convince *yourself* that you are worthy of serious consideration. One strategy to accomplish both aims is to find ways to strengthen your "credentials" and your credibility in the outside world while you are still in graduate school or employed as an academic.

If you have carefully assessed your skills in relation to your chosen field, you already know that you possess an impressive array of transferable skills and attributes. Nonetheless, some of you will start with credentials that are more directly relevant than will others. Social scientists or scientists with particular substantive expertise (e.g., economics, most applied sciences, area studies) or skills (e.g., statistics/econometrics, survey research, computer programming, experimental or lab techniques) may have kept their nonacademic options open all along and may even have a ready-made career path into a quasi-academic field. Humanists and "softer" social scientists, as well as others who change fields, will have to work harder at making a transition.

You can strengthen your case in several ways: by gaining work experience of various kinds, by taking pertinent courses or even returning to school, by reading the trade and professional literature, and by generally considering and countering the negative stereotypes you are likely to encounter as an academic trying to enter a particular profession. Finally, the way you present yourself through your resume and cover letters substantially affects your ability to change careers. Be sure to ask Career Advisers and other informational interviewees for advice on how best to strengthen your case.

Gaining Work Experience

Academics who have made a transition to nonacademic careers unanimously stress the importance of gaining relevant work experience by any feasible means. Through experience you gain the three C's: *credentials, credibility, and connections* (and/or "the foot in the door"). If you are still in graduate school, consider the following:

1. *Getting a summer job or internship* (paid if possible) in the field or organization you wish to enter. Paula DeMasi, a Ph.D. in Economics, energetically pursued this strategy: she worked as a consultant to the Chief Economist at the Bank of Boston for two summers, and took a fall leave of absence to do a paid internship at the International Monetary Fund, where she is now employed.

2. *Taking a part-time job or internship* during the academic year instead of teaching. Paula again furnishes an example, having worked as an Associate providing litigation support for Putnam, Hayes & Bartlett for one year during graduate school. It is not surprising that she had the luxury of choosing among eight job offers, several of which were from large consulting firms. Some graduate students have encountered employer resistance to taking on someone so "overqualified" as an intern. You will probably be more persuasive if you can offer to carry out a concrete project of value to the company.

3. *Volunteering* for an organization where you would like to be employed or that provides impressive credentials. This is still a primary route to nonprofit jobs and can be very effective in other sectors. For example, Vincent Cuccaro, an Assistant Professor of Italian, worked without pay for the Bank of Boston during his six-week intersession. He used that time to learn about international treasury operations, accomplish some useful research and writing projects for the bank, and have lunch with as many bank executives as possible. Vinnie impressed them with his ability to master concepts (which he viewed as simply learning another foreign language), his level of maturity and commitment, and his honesty; he was hired as a Management Trainee into the International Treasury Department, which he now heads.

4. *Freelancing or "consulting"* for targeted organizations (unpaid if necessary). Anthropologist Paul Dredge did both freelance consulting and writing in the area of corporate culture in order to "build his resume." This facilitated his move from an assistant professorship to an organizational development position at a Boston consulting company and, several years later, to his own consulting business.

5. *Writing articles* for newspapers, periodicals, or other relevant publications to build a portfolio. (This is especially important for aspiring writers, publicists, and artists.) Recall Steve Bennett (M.A., East Asian Studies) who boldly agreed to ghostwrite an article on a clinical chemistry topic for a corporate scientist; its publication launched his first career as a freelance science writer and editor.

6. *Getting international field experience.* This usually, but not always, refers to experience such as the Peace Corps in less developed countries, especially if you are interested in careers in international development. However, most international experience, including teaching English and translating, provides a valuable if not essential "credential" for international careers. For example, Nancy Pyle, a Ph.D. in Fine Arts, used her dissertation research experience in Turkey to her advantage in applying for a job as Director of the Mason Fellows Program, which brings Third-World, mid-career professionals to the Kennedy School of Government.

7. *Getting a postgraduate fellowship* in biotech or other high-tech companies or in government agencies or research institutions. Although most involve purely academic research, they can lead to a policy or

business career (recall Carol Farris) and a few offer a more direct link to the policy world.

If you are on leave or sabbatical or otherwise unfettered by a job (read: unemployed), you might seek a *"bridging" job*—one that will help give you the 3 C's as a springboard to the desired "real" position in the new field. For example, several GSAS alumni seeking jobs in business or consulting, including Dave Dyer and Alan Kantrow of the Winthrop Group, started with research and editing jobs at the Harvard Business School. Ellen Glew, a Ph.D. in German, whose long-range goal was to have her own international marketing services company, started her transition with Wang, in order to obtain broad experience in the industry and to build a network. Students looking for environmental careers find the Environmental Careers Organization, Inc. (formerly CEIP), which is headquartered in Boston, a valuable source of paid internships running from three to twelve months.

Your best source for part-time or full-time job possibilities is, as always, your network. In addition, OCS has numerous internship listings, as well as some job listings. In general, the job-search advice presented in the next chapter applies at this stage as well. Your task is actually easier at this point, because you are not seeking a long-term commitment and may not even be asking for pay. Rather, you are enlisting an ally in, as well as a beneficiary of, your determined quest to change careers.

Getting Additional Schooling/Training

For some fields, additional training and certification is absolutely necessary. If that is the case, your task is to find the best program for your needs, whether it is an in-house training program, a certification program, or a degree program. But don't assume you must go back full time to school because it's required or easier to make the transition; rather, look for ways to minimize and "informalize" the schooling. Most GSAS alumni who switched careers have done so without returning for another degree.

Instead, they often found that taking certain courses helped them make the transition—by providing them with *relevant skills* (e.g., financial accounting, computer programming, database/spreadsheet management, technical writing, editing), useful *substantive knowledge* (e.g., economics, organizational behavior, management, policy), the *vocabulary or "jargon"* of the field, and *evidence of their commitment* to the career change. As a GSAS student, you can easily take or audit courses elsewhere in the University, e.g., at the Business School, the Kennedy School, or the School of Education. Or you can consult the annual *Educational Opportunities of Greater Boston for Adults* to find other courses and certificate programs in the Boston area, such as those offered by the Boston Security Analysts Society. You can easily teach yourself some basic accounting with a programmed text such as Anthony's *Essentials of Accounting.* One innovative strategy is to find a place to teach a course in the area you wish to move into, as did two GSAS anthropologists who taught business school courses in marketing, or a history professor who taught business history. As you already know, the best way to learn a subject is to teach it.

Some companies provide their own training programs, such as the Bank of Boston's Loan Development Officer Training Program or Procter & Gamble's Brand Management training. In this case your challenge is to convince the company that you will fit in with the younger B.A.'s for whom the programs are usually designed. To take a specific example, Judith Garelick, a Ph.D. in English, was accepted by Baystate Financial Services into its training program for life insurance agents. In addition to attending seminars on all aspects of financial services, she was assigned a "professional trainer," who spent a full day a week in the field with her; he became her mentor and supported her eventual decision to create her own financial planning and brokerage business. Finally, you may even be sent to school by your employer; alumni examples include law school support for scientists hired to do patent work and grants or loans from consulting companies for M.B.A. programs. McKinsey and Company offers a mini-M.B.A. course for the Ph.D.'s it has begun to recruit.

Professional and trade associations also offer numerous formal and informal training opportunities, from short courses and panels to informal exchanges at meetings and other events. Use your personal contacts and the *Encyclopedia of Associations* to locate the relevant associations in your area.

Reading the Trade and Professional Literature

In many cases, you can teach yourself the vocabulary, concepts, and *Weltanschauung* of your new career field—a necessity for establishing credibility—by regularly reading trade and professional journals in your targeted field. Moreover, you can gain valuable clues about possible niches for you, industry/professional trends, promising organizational leads, and professional contacts. You've probably already sampled the trade and professional literature as part of the career exploration process. Assuming that you've narrowed and focused your career goals, you will want to read more extensively and consistently the "bibles" of your new field, e.g., for business: the *Wall Street Journal, Fortune, Forbes, Business Week*, and whatever specialty journals apply. (For suggestions in other fields, ask career advisers or acquaintances in Harvard professional schools what they read. Harvard students considering business careers can browse in the Cole Room at Baker Library at Harvard Business School.)

Countering Negative Stereotypes
Toward Graduate Students and Academics

Although the negative stereotypes of academics are much less pervasive now than they were a few years ago, you may still need to address them, both to reaffirm your initial assessment of workplace values and to counter any lingering concerns that potential employers may have about your ability to thrive in an "alien environment." They may be stereotypes but they are based on real differences between the two environments—particularly academic and business, which have been pointed out by more than one Career Adviser.

For example, Paul Blanchard, a Ph.D. in Astronomy and a consultant on strategic planning, executive leadership, and communication for the aerospace industry, points out actual—though often exaggerated—differences between academic and business work requirements, as follows:

	ACADEMIA	BUSINESS
workplace	(for tenured profs) artificial, stable, secure, shielded from competition	real world, changing, risky, subject to commercial forces
attitude twd. knowledge	pursued for own sake; goal: expertise	means to practical & organizational goals
time & info.	adequate for a good job; can "maximize," strive for certainty; most deadlines flexible	never enough; must "satisfice" (e.g., make decisions on 55% of desirable information); deadlines inflexible
primary interaction	people and data/info.	people, importance of collaboration, trust, confidence
primary work mode	autonomy within organization	teamwork within organization
personnel	shared background/ values	enormous diversity; less emphasis on academic credentials

Judy Esterquest notes some of the negative stereotypes of value differences in the two cultures in the chart on the following page.

Not only must graduate students persuade a potential employer in the business world that they do not fit the stereotype, they must also relinquish their own negative, often inaccurate stereotypes of the business world. Indeed, Judy Esterquest points to the *similarity* of some of the most negative labels each culture attaches to the other, such as: "Their environment requires absolute conformity"; "They think jargon has meaning"; "They are absurdly impressed by credentials"; "They define success too narrowly"; "They produce nothing of real value"; "They are arrogant"; "They don't value people; only ideas/numbers matter."

CONTRASTING STEREOTYPES

According to academics, **business people are:**	*According to business people,* **academics are:**
Mercenary	Simple-minded about money
Driven by time	Impractical about time
Non-reflective	Thought for thought's sake
Non-creative	Disorder proves creativity
Slick and superficial	Proudly unable to organize
No sense of standards	No sense of deadlines
Incapable of judging: People, projects, values	Incapable of judging: People, projects, money
Socially aggressive and intellectually passive	Socially passive and intellectually aggressive
Bottom line is everything	Armchair liberals
Tradeoffs always possible	Value ideals as absolutes
Everything is measured	Everything is judged

Consider both the real and imagined differences between the academic environment/culture and the one to which you aspire. Plan to demonstrate to potential employers how your training, experience, and temperament indicate an ability to navigate successfully in the new career field. You will impress them with your understanding of their field and may even "re-educate" them about academia. To bolster your confidence, bear in mind that GSAS Career Advisers rarely regret and always value their graduate education; and they genuinely believe it ultimately gives them an edge in their new careers. They relish telling stories about unexpected, seemingly esoteric skills gained in graduate school that transferred to their new field. Paul Dredge found that his fieldwork in Asia paid unexpected dividends in a new consulting project in Hong Kong, where he wrote on the flip charts in Chinese—to the applause of the clients.

Presenting Yourself:
C.V. to Resume, Cover Letters

The main purpose of resumes and cover letters at this stage of the process is to get you an interview with a potential employer. Put another way, they help you to organize, summarize, and highlight your experience and capacities as they relate to the job, in order to demonstrate credibility and attract interest. Resumes and cover letters are even more important for career changers than for those seeking jobs for which their training and experience prepares them. Although they provide only incomplete information that will be barely scanned, they are typically your only means to convince an employer to take a risk, at least to the point of interviewing you. Therefore, you need to tailor your presentation of skills, expertise, experience, and motivation to fit the requirements of the job or career you are seeking, while making the entire "package" irresistible. Alice Morgan, an English professor turned strategy consultant, puts it this way: "Find out what are considered good credentials [including experience] and lay claim to them. . . . In the absence of supporting evidence—which is, of course, the ideal—the next best thing is to *assert* that you can do it." [1] (This assumes that you believe you *can*

1. From a workshop on Nonacademic Careers, held at OCS, April 23, 1992.

do it. And, of course, you never lie about your credentials.) There's a real art to selling yourself with integrity and flair.

Resumes. Resumes require you to be both more concise and more general than c.v.'s, which display your academic credentials and accomplishments in great detail. Your resume will emphasize the experience and skills most relevant to the new career and probably downplay considerably your academic credentials and experience.

To begin the process, refer to your c.v., any old resumes, your self-assessment materials, job descriptions in your field, and the resume word list provided at the end of this chapter to generate *inclusive* lists: anything you can think of regarding your education, your paid *and* unpaid work experience, any important extracurricular and/or community activities, and skills and attributes related to work in the field you are targeting. By now you should have a good idea how your academic and other skills transfer to the new job and environment, so make the "translation" explicit in your lists. (If not, read job descriptions and advertisements in your field(s) of interest; jot down the phrases describing functions and requirements and match them with your list of skills.) For example, teaching might become: "training/presentation/communication skills," "facilitated small groups," "tutored/counseled individuals," "designed/wrote instructional materials," "evaluated written and verbal performance," "researched and selected materials," "coordinated and administered large course."

Write *concise descriptions* of what you did and accomplished in each job and activity, gearing them generally to the job descriptions. Use *active verbs* that communicate practicality and achievement (or "product"), in quantitative terms for business jobs, if possible. Include work that shows you completing projects, meeting deadlines, and performing other tasks pertinent to the new career area.

The next step is to cull out the most important and relevant material to include in your resume. To be concise, try combining less important but still advantageous items into a summary statement. You may need to create more than one version of your resume if you are applying for jobs in two different fields.

You should have a good sense from your informational network of the preferred forms and styles of resumes for the new profession or business. Several annotated examples are presented at the end of the chapter. The following are some generally applicable, common-sense rules:

1. Try to keep a resume to *one page*, particularly for business and media fields. If it goes to a second page, make sure the first page contains the essential information and the second page includes your name. Often you can present the second page as an addendum listing publications and like material.

2. Make the resume *visually effective to communicate professionalism and clarity*. Make it easy to scan as well, using CAPITAL LETTERS, **bold print**, *italics*, underlining, and spacing to highlight your strongest credentials. Don't make it too dense, busy, or cute. Use a high-quality, neutral color (preferably white or cream) bond paper (the same as for your cover letters). These stylistic choices are usually dictated by taste.

3. Be consistent in your use of grammatical structure and style, and avoid spelling and punctuation mistakes. PROOFREAD your resume several times and then have someone else proofread it as well. Use accurate, accessible language; avoid abbreviations and jargon—even those of your targeted career.

4. Be aware that information presented at the beginning of a section, at the left-hand margin, or in a column gets extra emphasis; therefore, it is generally *not* advisable to put dates in the margins. (Note, however, that dates in the margin appear to be de rigueur for Harvard M.B.A. resumes.) Items under "Education" and "Experience" are listed in reverse chronological order. Present information in order of its importance; for example, if you happen to have substantial experience or want to de-emphasize your doctorate, put experience before education. Or consider putting a skills summary first if that is your strongest point.

5. Select the best format for your qualifications and experience: reverse chronological, functional, or a combination. The *reverse chronological* is easier to construct and, as the most common type, is probably easier to "sell." It focuses on education and professional experience, starting with the most recent and working backward. *Functional formats* are most appropriate for people who have little related work experience or whose capabilities have been demonstrated in nonprofessional situations. Rather than listing experience chronologically by jobs, the functional resume categorizes your experience (including

paid and unpaid work and personal achievements) by skill, under functional subheads such as "Research and Writing," "Management," and "Teaching," followed by a brief section listing employment history. Functional resumes are harder to pull off successfully, partly because readers wonder if you are hiding something. For that reason, a *modified chronological resume* (see examples) is often more effective for career changers, especially if you want to emphasize skills in various areas for an all-purpose resume or to show variety of experience.

6. The usual categories of information include *Education, Experience or Professional Experience, Skills or Skills Summary, Activities or Community Service, Interests and Background* (or *Personal* or *Additional Information*). They are generally self-explanatory but are discussed in the annotations of the resume examples. Note that personal information such as age, marital status, health status, and race/ethnicity is omitted. Although citizenship or visa status information is not required, prudence might dictate including U.S. citizenship or permanent resident status if your nationality is ambiguous. (Foreign nationals should see Chapter 6.) Avoid "Job Objective" statements, because they usually sound vapid or canned and they can limit you unnecessarily. The same purpose—of helping the reader refer you to the logical position or people in the organization—is more effectively served in the cover letter.

7. References are usually omitted as well, and even the phrase "References furnished upon request" is often considered superfluous. However, before you go on the job market, you should line up your references—preferably not all academic. Explain what job(s) you are seeking and prime them (with a typed list perhaps) to emphasize skills and traits appropriate for that work. Sometimes—for example, if you have unusually strong, well-known, relevant recommenders—it is effective to list references, on a separate sheet. In the business world, if employers consult references at all, they tend to do it by telephone.

Cover letters. Having spent hours on your resume, you may be tempted to dash off the cover letter that goes with it. Resist the temptation! Remember that the cover letter will likely be the first thing the employer sees, whether he or she is the person specified by an ad you are answering or a targeted person whom you wish to ask about general opportunities in a specific organization. *Cover letters can be crucially important in getting you the interview* because they provide the means to highlight and elaborate your resume in response to a specific job, or at least to a specific type of job within a specific organization. Here, too, you can convey your enthusiasm and motivation for the particular job and organization, as well as other personal traits that relate to the job and your desirability as an employee and colleague. Indeed, you want to give the potential employer a sense of you as a person. Finally, your letter demonstrates your abilities to organize, write, and communicate.

Annotated examples of cover letters for various purposes (including information interviewing) are included at the end of the chapter. Here are some general rules to follow:

1. Type or laser print each letter on matching paper in a visually attractive, professional format. Make sure there are no spelling, grammatical, or punctuation errors, nor any errors of fact. Don't use abbreviations. Sign your name, above the typed version. Acceptable formats include: *full block* (every item fully left-aligned), *block* (left-aligned except for return address/date and complimentary closing/ signature), or *modified block* (same as block, but each paragraph is indented).

2. Address your letter to a specific individual if at all possible, particularly the one most likely to make a hiring decision. Be sure names and titles are correct. (If in doubt, call the organization and ask for names, titles, and spellings.)

3. Be concise; try to keep letters to one page, unless you have unusually extensive experience. Cover letters tend to be structured as follows:

   Paragraph 1 explains who you are (in a sentence) and why you are writing, using the name of a contact who referred you and/or the ad you are responding to, if applicable. You might summarize your interest and your conviction that this is a good match.

   Paragraphs 2 and 3 (possibly more) should communicate (in no particular order): (1) why you are interested in the field, organization/company, and job, and (2) what *value* you can offer them. Specifically refer to, and possibly elaborate on, experience from your resume by tailoring your description to the requirements of the job as you understand them. This is where you can capitalize on transferable skills, as well as point out character attributes desirable for the job.

In the closing paragraph you should express your intention to follow up with a phone call within a week or so and your hope that you can explore the possibility further in person. If you haven't done so already, you might express your enthusiasm. It never hurts to thank them for their consideration.

4. Write in a style that is natural for you, but keep in mind the dictates of professionalism. Avoid both the underuse and overuse of "I's," as well as the extremes of arrogance and self-deprecation. Humor catches attention but also carries risk. In sum, try to convey warmth, poise, maturity, and a little pizzazz.

Your strengths as a graduate student undoubtedly include persuasiveness, an ability to write, attention to detail, and perfectionism. Apply them in producing your resume and cover letters, so you do not give potential employers an excuse to screen you out as an applicant. That brings us to the next phase of the process—searching and applying for actual jobs.

RESUME WORD LISTS

Verbs that Describe Your Functional Skills

Accelerated	Coached	Detected	Followed
Achieved	Collaborated	Determined	Forecast
Accomplished	Collected	Developed	Formed
Acted	Communicated	Devised	Formulated
Activated	Combined	Diagnosed	Founded
Adapted	Compared	Directed	Framed
Added	Competed	Documented	Gathered
Addressed	Compiled	Doubled	Gave
Administered	Completed	Drove	Generated
Advised	Composed	Earned	Got
Allocated	Computed	Edited	Governed
Analyzed	Conceived	Effected	Guided
Anticipated	Concluded	Elicited	Halved
Appointed	Condensed	Eliminated	Handled
Approved	Conducted	Empathized	Headed
Arranged	Constructed	Employed	Helped
Ascertained	Contacted	Enforced	Hired
Assembled	Controlled	Engineered	Identified
Assessed	Coordinated	Established	Illustrated
Assisted	Copied	Estimated	Implemented
Attained	Counseled	Evaluated	Improvised
Audited	Crafted	Examined	Increased
Augmented	Created	Executed	Indexed
Bought	Cultivated	Expanded	Influenced
Briefed	Dealt	Expedited	Initiated
Broadened	Debated	Experimented	Inspected
Built	Decentralized	Explained	Instituted
Calculated	Decided	Extracted	Instructed
Centralized	Decreased	Fabricated	Insured
Changed	Defined	Facilitated	Interpreted
Chartered	Delegated	Fashioned	Interviewed
Checked	Delivered	Filed	Introduced
Clarified	Demonstrated	Financed	Invented
Classified	Designed	Fixed	Inventoried

Invested	Persuaded	Resolved	Trained
Investigated	Photographed	Restored	Translated
Judged	Piloted	Reversed	Trimmed
Kept	Pioneered	Reviewed	Tutored
Launched	Planned	Revised	Typed
Learned	Predicted	Revitalized	Uncovered
Lectured	Prepared	Saved	Understood
Led	Presented	Scheduled	Unified
Lifted	Prevented	Searched	Unraveled
Listened	Processed	Selected	Used
Located	Procured	Separated	Utilized
Logged	Produced	Served	Verbalized
Made	Programmed	Serviced	Verified
Maintained	Promoted	Settled	Visualized
Managed	Proposed	Shaped	Vitalized
Manipulated	Proved	Simplified	Widened
Marketed	Provided	Sold	Won
Measured	Publicized	Solved	Worked
Mediated	Published	Staffed	Wrote
Memorized	Purchased	Started	
Met	Questioned	Stimulated	
Minimized	Raised	Streamlined	
Mobilized	Read	Stretched	
Modeled	Realized	Structured	
Modernized	Reasoned	Studied	
Monitored	Received	Summarized	
Negotiated	Recommended	Supervised	
Networked	Reconciled	Supported	
Observed	Recorded	Supplied	
Obtained	Recruited	Surpassed	
Offered	Redesigned	Surveyed	
Operated	Reduced	Synthesized	
Ordered	Regulated	Systematized	
Organized	Referred	Talked	
Originated	Renegotiated	Taught	
Painted	Reorganized	Terminated	
Participated	Repaired	Tested	
Perceived	Reported	Tightened	
Performed	Represented	Traced	
Persevered	Researched	Traded	

Adaptive Skill Words That Describe
Your Personal Traits

Active	Humorous
Adaptable	Innovative
Adept	Instrumental
Broad-minded	Logical
Competent	Loyal
Conscientious	Mature
Creative	Methodical
Dependable	Objective
Determined	Outgoing
Diplomatic	Personable
Disciplined	Pleasant
Discreet	Positive
Efficient	Productive
Energetic	Reliable
Enterprising	Resourceful
Experienced	Self-reliant
Fair	Sensitive
Forceful	Sincere
Forthright	Successful
Honest	Tactful

SAMPLE RESUMES AND COVER LETTERS

Note: These resumes appear more cramped than they were in the originals because of the page size constraints. In some cases, they are slightly distorted as well as downsized. All addresses and all but two names have been changed.

MAXWELL NEWMAN
Prescott Street, Apt. 0
Cambridge, Massachusetts 02138
Telephone: 617/123-4567

EDUCATION

Harvard University, Ph.D., Computer Science, 1989.
M.A., Mathematics, 1987.
University of Oregon, B.A., Mathematics, 1983.
Honors, Phi Beta Kappa.
MIT, Intensive 6-month CS program, 1981.

PROFESSIONAL EXPERIENCE

Bell Laboratories, Microsoft, Bull, Matra, Interleaf, Camex, et al.
Ten years in the computer industry, 1981-1991.

Product design and development
- Designed and built a prototype of a fault-tolerant database file server. Proved the most successful product introduction of the company—over 100 units in one quarter at an 80% markup.
- Conceived and built a system to port a 100,000-line program to new platforms fast, below cost.
- Built an X.25 layer in an OS for a French firm.
- Designed a network protocol now shipped in Microsoft OS products.
- Ran a team of six to build a computer vision software facility at Harvard.
- Designed a graphics editing and sequencing system now in everyday use in the French Videotex industry.

Systems expertise
- DEC, SUN, IBM, and Apple, micros to super-minis.
- UNIX, MS-DOS. Languages from ucode to C and LISP.
- Advised in over $1 million of computer equipment purchases.

Feasibility studies
- Created procedures to evaluate computer components (i.e., disks, laser graphics scanners) to give R&D management informed choices.
- Prototyped a digital telephone message editor, precursor to voice mail.
- Evaluated performance of hardware configurations to find cost-effective replacement components and suggested new technology development.

Manufacturing procedures
- Streamlined manufacturing of a dedicated database machine.
- Built a highly cost-effective automated test system that used a known working unit to test units coming off the line.

Organization
- Managed a one-week seminar in Hokkaido, Japan, with a team of three Japanese and two U.S. coordinators. Handled applications procedures, coordinated travel, and supervised day-to-day activities of 61 participants and six guest lecturers on a $250,000 budget.

RELATED SKILLS AND EXPERIENCE

Languages:	fluent French, basic German.
Teaching experience:	AI, Computer Vision, UNIX workshops, Calculus
Experience abroad:	France-19 mos., Yugoslavia-2 mos., Japan-2 mos.

This functional resume is effective because Max has both training and work experience in the field he wants to enter. He conveys both accomplishments and skills in his Professional Experience and cleverly bundles his other skills and experiences together at the end. A Work History section would be helpful, but the tradeoff was keeping the resume to one page. Note that bullets tend to be popular in business fields.

VINEER BHANSALI

HOME ADDRESS
Leverett House X-00
25 DeWolfe Street
Cambridge, MA 02138
(617) 493-0000

OFFICE ADDRESS
Jefferson Physical Labs.
Harvard University
Cambridge, MA 02138
(617) 495-0000
E-Mail: xxxxxx@huhepi

EDUCATION

Harvard University	Ph.D.	Theoretical Particle Physics	1992
Caltech	M.S. with Honor	Physics	1987
Caltech	B.S. with Honor	Physics, Math, and Astronomy	1987

(The B.S. and M.S. degrees were awarded simultaneously after three years of study. GPA 4.2; A=4.0)

| Brown University | Theoretical Advanced Study Institute | 1988 |

FELLOWSHIPS AND HONORS

Harvard University: Goldhaber Prize in Graduate Physics (1987-88); Distinction in teaching, Bok Center for Teaching and Learning (1990,91); Graduate Student Council Conference Travel Grant (1992).

Caltech: Carnation Merit Prize (1987); TIME magazine College Achievement Award (1987); Haren Lee Fisher Memorial Physics Prize (1987); ASCIT teaching prize (1987); Summer Undergraduate Research Fellowships (1986,87, details in publication list); Tau Beta Pi; Sigma Xi.

Other: National Mathematics Olympiad Gold Medal, India (1984).

PUBLICATIONS
(Please refer to attached list)

RESEARCH EXPERIENCE AND SKILLS

Doctoral Dissertation: "Symmetries, Anomalies and Effective Field Theory" (1992); Advisors: Howard Georgi, Sidney Coleman, Sheldon Glashow, Eric Carlson (all at Harvard).

Master's Theoretical Research: "Factorizable S Matrices" (1987); Advisor: Richard Feynman (Caltech).

Experimental Senior Thesis: "In-Situ Sheet Resistivity Measurements in MeV Damaged Gallium Arsenide" (1987); Advisor: Thomas Tombrello (Caltech).

Computer Science: Extensive Programming experience in C on the Caltech Nearest Neighbor Concurrent Processor dealing with problems in statistics, graphics and lattice gauge theories (1984-87); Advisor: Geoffrey C. Fox (Caltech). Also experienced with numerical methods, system management, Fortran, Pascal and C++.

TEACHING EXPERIENCE
(Please refer to addendum for details.)

Harvard University: *Teaching Consultant* for the Bok Center for Teaching and Learning (1990-92); *Teaching Fellow* (1987-92) in advanced graduate courses (Quantum Field Theory, Microphysical Cosmology), upper level undergraduate courses (Quantum Mechanics, Classical Mechanics, Real Analysis, Applications of Quantum Theory) and introductory courses (Principles of Physics in Harvard College and Harvard Extension School); *Resident Tutor* in Physics in Dudley and Leverett Houses of Harvard College (1990-92).

Caltech: *Undergraduate Teaching Assistant* in Quantum Mechanics and Real Analysis (1986-87)

ACTIVITIES AND INTERESTS

NCAA division 3 Tennis, Southern California (Varsity letterman at Caltech 1984-87). Under-21 National School Cricket Team, India (1982-84). Undergraduate Admissions Representative for Caltech (1989-92).

LANGUAGES

Fluent in English, Hindi, Sanskrit. Reasonable skills in Italian and Spanish.

INVITED PROFESSIONAL SEMINAR PRESENTATIONS

XXVI International Conference on High Energy Physics, Dallas, TX (Aug. 1992); *XIX International Colloquium in Group Theoretical Methods in Physics*, Salamanca, Spain (June 1992); *Harmonic Oscillator Workshop*, College Park, Maryland (March 1992); *Mathematical Physics Seminar*, CRM, University of Montreal, Montreal, Canada (Oct. 1991); Parallel session at *Second International Wigner Symposium*, Goslar, Germany (July 1991); *Research Seminar*, Tata Institute of Fundamental Research, Bombay, India (July 1989, July 1990, June 1992); *D.S.T. Workshop in Particle Physics*, 'Superstring Theory,' I.I.T., Kanpur, India (Dec. 1987).

Vineer used this resume in a successful quest for investment banking jobs (as you will see in Chapter 6). He appended a page listing his publications and a second listing his teaching experience in detail. Note that he omits reference to his Indian citizenship. Although the resume is dense, his use of graphics makes it fairly easy to scan. The original was on one page and the Invited Professional Seminar Presentations section appeared after Teaching Experience.

Lucas McGovern
Pleasant Street
Cambridge, MA 02138
(617) 491-0000

EDUCATION

HARVARD UNIVERSITY. Ph.D., Music Composition, 1989.
Dissertation, String Quartet No. 1.

NEW ENGLAND CONSERVATORY OF MUSIC. MM, with Honors, 1983. BM, 1980.

EXPERIENCE

ENTREPRENEURIAL/MANAGERIAL

Co-Founder (1983) and currently **President** of NuClassix, Inc., a nonprofit, tax-exempt corporation that launches the careers of gifted composers. Managed transformation of NuClassix from an ad hoc group of composers to a growing public service organization through the creation and implementation of a multi-board organizational structure. Directed successful fundraising efforts generating over $100,000. Organized senior staff search.

Founder and Manager of Lucas McGovern Quartet, a small music performance business, 1980-1988. Conceived and conducted all marketing, contracting, and client relations for a four-piece jazz band. Built annual billings to over $25,000. Developed successful marketing strategy based on product differentiation (high-level jazz and swing performance) and specific market focus.

Purchased, with partner, three-unit residential income property. Established accounting procedures to control liquidity and debt obligations. Hired contractors and supervised major renovations. Managed rental income and tenant relations during a two-year period when income was improved by 31.25%. Cut costs by 3.33%.

TEACHING

Lecturer on Music, HARVARD UNIVERSITY, 1989-present

Teaching Fellow in Music, HARVARD UNIVERSITY, 1985-1989. Taught sections in common practice theory, Beethoven symphonies, opera, and jazz history. Awarded Oscar Schafer Scholarship in recognition of an "extensive and outstanding contribution to the teaching of music." Jazz Studies Faculty, New England Conservatory of Music, 1983-1984.

ACTIVITIES

MUSIC
Composed and met production deadlines for 15 new works over six years. Performances throughout New England and New York including Alice Tully Hall at Lincoln Center, by such groups as the Vermont Symphony, New World String Quartet, Middlebury College Choir, and NuClassix. Numerous radio interviews. Numerous awards for creative work including ASCAP Foundation Grant, 1st Prize Blodgett Composers Competition, and George Knight Prize. String Quartet #1 available on compact disc. Extensive performance as jazz pianist.

COMMUNITY
Organized and helped establish Ronan Park Neighbors Association, a community group dedicated to improving area living conditions.

LANGUAGES
Reading German.

In seeking a major career change into business or nonprofit development, Lucas effectively expands and highlights his entrepreneurial experience within music in this modified functional resume.

M. CYNTHIA DELDON

Local Address
00 Irwin St.
Cambridge, MA 02138
(617) 888-1111

Permanent Address
111 Cedar Rd.
Eastern, MA 01434
(301) 888-8888

EDUCATION

HARVARD UNIVERSITY   Cambridge, MA
MA, East Asian Studies, expected February 1992
East Asian Studies Department Research Grant, Summer 1991

NANZAN UNIVERSITY   Nagoya, Japan
Rotary Foundation Graduate Scholar, 1988-89

GEORGETOWN UNIVERSITY   Washington, DC
BA, History, May 1987
East Asian Studies Certificate, School of Foreign Service
Junior Year Abroad, Sophia University, Tokyo, Japan

EXPERIENCE

U.S. EMBASSY   Tokyo, Japan
Intern, Political Section. Assignments modelled on responsibilities of junior foreign service officers. These included drafting weekly political reports sent to the State Department, researching and writing a study on the politics of the agricultural lobby in Japan, orchestrating and updating biographical files on Japanese political leaders, staffing and drafting official reports on Tokyo meetings of the U.S. Assistant Secretary of State, and assisting the Political Minister at internal and external meetings. Summer 1991

MINISTRY OF INTERNATIONAL TRADE AND INDUSTRY   Tokyo, Japan
Special Assistant to the Minister. Acted as the Minister's primary adviser on international protocol and English language translation and correspondence. In addition, attended and reported on LDP policy meetings, represented the Minister at political rallies and meetings with his constituents, and participated in conferences with staff of the Research Institute of MITI. Fall 1990

THE SAINT PAUL'S SCHOOL   Concord, NH
Teaching Intern, Advanced Studies Program. Taught high school seniors Japanese language and culture. Summer 1990

U.S. CHAMBER OF COMMERCE   Washington, DC
International Affairs Program Assistant. Assisted the Director of South Asian Affairs in developing and implementing the Chamber's policies and programs in Southeast Asia. Primary responsibilities included administering the U.S.-India Business Council (a bilateral policy organization comprised of fifty Fortune 500 companies), monitoring and analyzing U.S.-India commercial relations and related trade legislation, coordinating international business conferences in India, and drafting evaluations and reports for projects administered by the Center for International Private Enterprise (CIPE), a Chamber of Commerce affiliate devoted to promoting private enterprise abroad. Work required extensive interaction in the U.S. and India with government and business leaders. August 1987-July 1988

PERSONAL

Languages Fluent in Japanese (First Place, Consulate General of Japan Speech Contest, April 1990)
Proficient in French (Semester Abroad, Lycée Audiberte, Antibes, France, 1983)

Travel Japan, Korea, Malaysia, Singapore, China, Hong Kong, India, and extensive travel throughout Europe.

Cynthia was seeking a job that utilized her expertise in East Asian studies (particularly Japan) in a business or nonprofit setting. Because all her work experience was related in some way to this objective, she could use the traditional reverse chronology format to advantage. Her languages (note the evidence provided) and travel are also highly relevant. She got a job at the Asian Society, through a networking contact. The original was on one page; it is expanded here for readability.

HANNAH A. LAMPMAN
000 Memphis Drive, Number 000
Cambridge, Massachusetts 02138
(617) 555-1234

PUBLIC RELATIONS/MANAGEMENT EXPERIENCE

Earth Day Cambridge. Directed radio publicity and wrote public service campaigns. Arranged and participated in on-air interviews (1990).

Cambridge River Festival. Recruited and managed 100 volunteers. Tripled income from merchandise sales (1989).

Mobilia Gallery. Designed displays, sold pieces, organized shows, directed publicity (1988).

DeCordova Museum/Brockton Museum. Created and organized a wearable art fashion show for joint exhibit (1987).

ACADEMIC EXPERIENCE

Boston University. Department of Modern Foreign Languages, Lecturer in Spanish (1985-1986).

Harvard University. Department of Romance Languages and Literatures, Lecturer in Advanced Spanish and Spanish Literature. (1981-1983).

University of Nevada at Reno. Department of Foreign Languages, Lecturer in Spanish and Spanish Literature (1976-1979).

Wellesley College. Spanish Department, Lecturer in Spanish and Spanish Literature (1975-1976).

Harvard University. Department of Romance Languages and Literatures, Teaching Fellow in Advanced Spanish (1971-1975).

University of California at Santa Barbara. Department of Spanish and Portuguese, Teaching Assistant in Spanish (1969-1971).

EDUCATION

Harvard University. Ph.D. in Romance Languages and Literatures (1983).
University of California at Santa Barbara. M.A. in Spanish Literature (1971).
University of California at San Diego. B.A. in Literature: Spanish and French (1969).

LANGUAGES

Fluent in Spanish and French. Lived four years in Greece, two in Bolivia, two in Tunisia, one in Taiwan and one in Spain.

Hannah sought a position in fundraiser/events coordinating and/or public relations for an environmental organization. She heads her resume with her somewhat limited but crucial volunteer experience, downplaying both her academic experience and credentials (the latter partly because of the time elapsed since her degrees). Hannah first did volunteer work in recycling, which led to a paid job as the Assistant Coordinator at Cambridge Recycling.

Anna Limb
00 Highland Avenue
Somerville, MA 02143
(617) 666-7777

Education

HARVARD UNIVERSITY — Doctoral candidate, English Literature and Language. M.A., 1988.

UNIVERSITY OF PENNSYLVANIA — B.A., *cum laude*, English Literature, 1987.

KING'S COLLEGE, LONDON — Won the Medieval Prize in English Faculty, 1985/86.

Experience

Teaching Fellow HARVARD UNIVERSITY   Cambridge, MA
Taught sections in the English Department and the Core Program and supervised two junior tutorials. Led discussion sections, graded papers and exams, and worked with students individually on a reading course culminating in the junior essay. 1990-1991.

Research Assistant HARVARD UNIVERSITY, Dept. of English   Cambridge, MA
Worked on Professor Larry D. Benson's planned *Concordance to Chaucer*. Rewrote and designed the *Pronunciation Guide to Chaucer* used within the university by several hundred students each year. Also recorded part of the tape which accompanies the *Guide*. 1989-90.

Staff Writer INDEPENDENT BOOK PROJECT
Researched material, wrote first draft and oversaw the early stages of production for projected book on children's games. Included hiring an illustrator and setting up production deadlines. Summer 1989.

Public Relations Consultant LEXICOM   Cambridge, MA
Promoted DesignSystems (now Imprimatur/DesignSystems), a graphic design firm. Published articles concerning the firm, directly or indirectly, in the Ventura newsletter and *EP&P*; secured their first assignment from *Publish!* magazine, which has developed into a steady business relationship. Also capitalized on the publicity accompanying the release of PhotoMac by promoting DesignSystems' cover image. The press release I wrote for PhotoMac's promotion folder was followed up by pieces in *Verbum* and *Personal Publishing*. Summer 1988.

Editorial Assistant FOREIGN POLICY RESEARCH INSTITUTE Philadelphia, PA
Participated in every phase of text production for *ORBIS*, a journal of foreign affairs, published quarterly. Copyedited from finishing touches to complete overhauls; met deadlines; and dealt with printers, typesetting codes and authors. 1986-87.

Recorder for the Blind SIX YEARS VOLUNTEER EXPERIENCE
Recorded *The Diary of Anne Frank* for the permanent collection of the Regional Library for the Blind and Physically Handicapped in Philadelphia; also one of the team that recorded *Playboy* for the Library of Congress. Worked on textbooks at the Royal Institute for the Blind in London. Reader at Recording for the Blind in Cambridge.

Other Skills

Excellent French, reading knowledge of German. Familiar with desktop publishing systems; willing to travel.

June 20, 1992

John Smith
Vice President
CEO Partnership, P.C.
Suite 222
Boulder, Colorado 80203

Dear Mr. Smith:

I read your letter to Carolann Brockett in the Office of Career Services at Harvard, and I can scarcely imagine another human being more suitable to your requirements. I have degrees from *two* Ivy league schools; of course I'm good-looking; but more importantly, I am energetic, eager to learn, creative and committed (not to mention courteous, kind, loyal...etc.).

My writing skills are excellent; I am not only consistently grammatical and coherent, but concise and versatile. I can do *The Decline and Fall of the Roman Empire* or trashy novel-ese as required. As for acquaintance with desktop publishing, this letter was produced in TEX and printed with a Canon laserjet. I am also familiar with PageMaker and Ventura.

On top of all of this, I am seeking a place to live where the summers are cool and the humidity is low. If you are interested, I will be more than happy to forward writing samples and references. For now, I include only my resume. I do hope this job is still available and that we can discuss it further.

Sincerely,

Anna Limb

Anna sought work in the media field—PR, writing, editing—to test career alternatives during an extended leave of absence from graduate school. She highlights her relevant work experience within a chronological format by setting off her titles in the margin. She achieves an effective, clean look mainly through the use of capital letters, italics, and spacing.

Both her cover letters won her interviews, but she got the job at CEO Partnership, to whom she wrote a high-risk letter! If you choose to write such a letter, be aware that it could alienate *at least* as easily as it could charm. Given her knowledge of the job and submission of writing samples, her letter to Temple, Barker & Sloane is appropriately longer than most cover letters, and it ultimately led to a freelance job there.

June 22, 1992

Ms. Rachel Seaver
Director of Writing/Editing
Temple, Barker & Sloane
12 Holder St.
Nebraska

Dear Ms. Seaver:

I am looking for a career that will allow me to use and develop my skills as writer, editor and adviser. I want variety in my day-to-day work and the chance to learn about many different fields.

I spoke with Mike Walsh on Tuesday about the work he does at Temple, Barker & Sloane, and it seems as if the Writing/Editing department and I could make a perfect match. Mike referred me to you and suggested I enclose some writing samples. The short pieces I have included give a fairly good indication of the kind of writing work I can do. Let me put them in context a bit for you.

• The first is a short article from *EP&P* on designing fonts electronically, which I co-authored with David Dobrin, my former boss at Lexicom. The article was conceived and written as part of a publicity drive for DesignSystems, a small graphic design firm in Cambridge. Besides writing, I researched the history of typography, arranged for the use of the Dürer engraving from the Metropolitan Museum and convinced Jonathan Jackson to design Uglyfont, which is now included on the master list of commercial fonts.

• Next is a press release that I persuaded the PR people at Avalon to include in their information folder on the press tour that accompanied the release of PhotoMac, a color-separation program for the MAC. DesignSystems was responsible for PhotoMac's particularly striking cover image, which even made it to the cover of a computing magazine.

• Third is the first few pages of "Some Notes on Chaucer's Language." As research assistant to Professor Larry Benson at Harvard, my job was to overhaul the original *Pronunciation Guide to Chaucer*, which was correct as far as it went but nearly unreadable and dull. I wish I had a copy of the densely typewritten columns I started out with for you to see. I devised the new format with clean tables, loosened up the grammatical explanations and introduced the illustrative examples from passages in Chaucer. The current version is distributed to some four hundred students each year and sent to various schools across the country upon request.

I have a good deal of experience with copyediting, which comes from my work on *ORBIS*, the journal of the Foreign Policy Research Institute, and from collaboration with David Dobrin. I edited his book, *Writing and Technique*, in manuscript, and he still calls on me occasionally to go over articles and proposals.

As a teaching fellow at Harvard this past year, part of my job was to supervise two Honors concentrators in what is called the junior tutorial. I worked individually with each student to devise a practical and thorough reading course in the fall semester which would contribute to and culminate in the junior essay in the spring. I spent a lot of time discussing their ideas and refining them until they reached a point where they could settle on a critical approach and organization for themselves. On the technical end, we set up interim deadlines for completed research and drafts, and both of my students ended up writing very good papers. I found that this was my favorite part of teaching and the thing I most want to continue doing.

The Writing/Editing department demands many of the abilities which have been my strongest in the past. I can do research and write; work with others to improve their writing; make the writing I'm associated with as good as it can be. And I want to use these skills in the challenging environment of a consulting firm. I would like to talk more about this in person. I will call in a few days to see what you think.

Sincerely,

Anna Limb

Tessa Nosaka

00 Francisco Avenue, Apt. 00
Cambridge, MA 02138
(617) 490-2222

EDUCATION

Harvard University, Doctoral Program, Comparative Religions
Tuition Fellowship (1990-1992); Junior Fellow, Center for the
Study of World Religions (Fall 1990)

Harvard Divinity School, Masters of Divinity, June 1987
Tuition Fellowship (1983-1986); Hopkins Shareholder 1987
(Honor awarded by the faculty to six graduating seniors)

Stanford University, Bachelor of Arts, Japanese, 1973

International Christian University, Mitaka, Japan, 1968-1970

PROFESSIONAL EXPERIENCE

INTERCULTURAL/INTERNATIONAL
Established and oversaw institution-wide educational and cultural
programming. Initiated and implemented prejudice reduction and
leadership training for students. Counseled and advocated for Asian/
African-American and Latina students. Served as college representative on Governing Council, Society Organized Against Racism.

WRITING/EDITING
Freelance editor and writer.
Author: *The Yamato Colony,* essays, and poetry.
Archival and field researcher.
Editor of quadrilingual newsletter.
Writer of press releases, informational handouts, and donor reports.

PUBLIC SPEAKING
Resource person and speaker on issues of race and identity; the
intersection of religion, gender, and culture; Japan and Japanese
Americans.
  • MIT Women's Studies Conference
  • Mt. Holyoke College
  • Lesley College
  • Women's Theological Center
  • Asian Women Theologians
  • Japan Society of Boston
  • New England Japanese American Citizen's League

ADMINISTRATIVE
Established systems and supervised administration of student health
insurance program. Coordinated and wrote departmental publicity.
Served as departmental representative on college committees and
task forces.

Tessa effectively presents the various related areas of her competence in this
functional resume, providing a work history on the second page (in contrast to Max
Newman). She makes good use of various graphics and makes sure the most important
information is on the first page.

WORK HISTORY

Harvard University, The Pluralism Project, Cambridge, MA
    Research Assistant, Summer 1991
Lesley College, Office of Student Affairs, Cambridge, MA
    Student Services Assistant, 1987-1990
East Boston Ecumenical Council, Boston, MA
    Intern, 1985-1986
Harvard/Radcliffe Financial Aid Office, Cambridge, MA
    Writer, Summer 1985
St. Elizabeth's Hospital, Brighton, MA
    Intensive training in pastoral care and counseling, Summer
    1984
Ask Inc., Tokyo, Japan
    Freelance Writer, 1981
PAOS Inc., Tokyo, Japan
    Freelance Writer, 1982
Sankei International College, Tokyo, Japan
    English Instructor, Spring 1982
Japanese American Citizens League, Livingston, CA
    Commissioned Author, 1974-1980

PUBLICATIONS

The Yamato Colony (1981)
"Growing Up Asian" (*Making Waves*, Beacon Press, 1989)
Poetry and Essays: *Greenfield Review, Sojourner, Stone Lion Review,*
    Japan Times, Friends Journal, Mainichi Weekly

LANGUAGES

Japanese, New Testament Greek, Theological French

References furnished upon request.

In her cover letter applying for an academic administrative/student services job, Tessa highlights her skills, experience—both personal and professional—and her values as they relate to the job as she understands it. (Note that this is the exceptional case where religious preference is relevant.) This letter resulted in an interview. She later found a job in student services (with responsibilities for multicultural affairs) in an elite university.

00 Ellis Ave., Rm. 00
Cambridge, MA 02138
May 20, 1990

Ms. Patricia Simpson
Manager of Employee Relations
Wellesley College
Wellesley, MA 02181

Dear Ms. Simpson:

I am writing to you to apply for the position of Dean of Religious Life at Wellesley College.

I graduated from Harvard Divinity School in 1987. My Master's of Divinity thesis presented a Japanese American feminist exploration of shrine Shinto and a reflection on a context of faith in the resolution of conflicts of identity.

Following graduation from Harvard, I spent three years at Lesley College in Student Affairs, where I initiated new programming intended to build community within the institution and to extend and develop ties within the neighborhood and the Greater Boston area. Under my leadership, committees of faculty, students, and staff extended Women's History observations from a week to a month; similar committees developed celebrations and events focusing on Black History, Asian New Years, and cultural diversity. Three important aspects of my work were: a concern for the institution's ideals of inclusivity and empowerment, active attempts to involve all members of the institution, and use of the arts. In 1989, Women's History Month culminated in an art show, reading, and literary journal, all featuring works by students, faculty, and staff. A "Wisdom Wheel" was also unveiled—mounted on a special frame designed and built by the college's carpenter, highlighting women's wisdom, announced by a women's drumming group, and featuring cloth panels made by undergraduates and graduate students, support staff, young people learning independent living skills in Lesley's Threshold Program, faculty, etc.

In subsequent work in the doctoral program in religion at Harvard, I have focused on religious pluralism in the United States and on our theological and concrete responses to it. Last summer, I investigated the history and current state of Buddhism in Boston, meeting with both Asian-born and American-born Buddhists in this area. Later, I traveled to Stockton, California for an examination of religious pluralism there. (My final report discussed Stockton's Sikh gurdwara, Jodo Shinshu Buddhist Church, and Shinto shrine.)

I believe that my experiences and skills particularly suit me for the Wellesley position. Though I lacked the formal title, I always considered my work at Lesley a chaplaincy. I am a Sansei (third generation Japanese American) feminist—a Quaker and the grandniece of a Shinto priest. I anchor myself within a multi-traditional religious frame. I am also keenly aware that true community is built upon tension. Grounding ourselves in an affirmation of commonality, we must also learn to see and respect particularity. I envision the Dean as a person charged to help the institution grapple with this tension as it works to fulfill its educational ideals.

Sincerely,

Tessa Nosaka

MARY E. HELMSLEY

00 Divider St.   Center for International Affairs
Newport, RI 02918   Harvard University
(401) 888-9999   1737 Cambridge St.
                                                          Cambridge, MA 02138

EDUCATION

Ph.D., Political Science, Harvard University, 1990
M.A., Political Science, Harvard University, 1982
B.A., Political Science, University of California, Berkeley, 1976 (Phi Beta Kappa)

Trained in the political, economic, and financial relations between advanced
industrial and less developed countries; development; and African politics.
Dissertation: "Crisis, Constraints, and State-Society Relations: The Politics of
African Economic Adjustment in the 1980's."

TEACHING

Instructor, Political Science, University of Illinois, Champaign-Urbana. 1987-88
Instructor, Government, Hamilton College, Clinton, NY. Fall 1985
Teaching Fellow, Government, Harvard University. 1978-84

Taught courses on the political economy of development, African politics,
comparative politics, and international relations.

RESEARCH

Associate, Center for International Affairs, Harvard. 1989-90
Visiting Scholar, Department of Political Science and Center for African Studies,
University of Illinois. Summer 1985, 1986
Research Assistant to Professor Stephan Haggard, Harvard. Wrote reports on six
African countries' experiences with the IMF's Extended Fund Facility. 1983-84
Research Assistant to Professor Joel Migdal, Harvard. Helped prepare manuscript
for publication; assisted in research on state-society relations. 1977-78

BUSINESS AND ADMINISTRATION

Assistant Chair, Africa Seminar, Center for International Affairs, Harvard.
Contacted speakers, organized publicity. 1989-90
Director of Marketing and Distribution, Ralph Arlyck Films, Poughkeepsie, NY.
Devised and implemented new marketing strategies for films of independent
filmmaker. 1984-85
Administrative Assistant, Center for International Affairs, Harvard.
Collected information on the activities of the Center and its associates. Produced
the working draft of the 1980-82 Biennial Report. Summer 1982
Skip-tracer, University of California Student Loan Office. Summer 1976

SKILLS   Languages: French, reading ability in Spanish
          Quantitative: Statistical analysis

TRAVEL   Kenya (6 weeks, predissertation research); Egypt; Mexico; Western Europe
          (included living with French family for 10 days)

Here is an example of moving from academia (where teaching has apparently slowed
down the dissertation writing process) to targeted positions in business, making use
of her substantive expertise. Because of this and the limitations of her business
experience, Mary begins with her education and her academic experience. The last
third of the resume highlights experience and skills more directly related to her goals.
Graphically, the resume is simple but effective.

March 13, 1990

Mr. Nick Holt
President and CEO
Equator Holdings, Ltd.
Equator House
111 Charter Oak Ave.
Hartford, CT 06106

Dear Mr. Holt:

I am writing to inquire about the possibility of working at Equator. I am currently an Associate at the Center for International Affairs and a Ph.D. candidate in Government at Harvard. My training is in international political economy and African development, and my own work is on African debt and the politics of adjustment in Africa. I expect to complete my academic work by the end of this summer, so I am looking for a position starting in the fall.

Although you may not remember, we met about three years ago at Lake Cumberland, Kentucky. I was at the Patterson School's Board of Advisors meeting because my husband, Andrew Ross, had just started teaching at UK and was associated with the Patterson School. Meeting you and hearing you speak was my first introduction to Equator, and I have kept it in mind since then as a place where I might be able to make a contribution, participate actively in African economic affairs, and make productive use of my training.

My background has given me a base of knowledge and skills needed in a company that conducts business with Africa. I understand the current economic crisis, African policy responses, political pressures, and interactions with international financial institutions, all of which are crucial elements of the business environment in the 1990s. In addition, I believe that the analytical tools I have developed would allow me to transfer my understanding quickly into a business setting.

My administrative and business experience includes managing the marketing and distribution of educational films for a freelance filmmaker, and this year I have been helping to run the Africa Seminar at the Center for International Affairs. Most of my work experience has been in university teaching, from which I have acquired valuable skills in communicating with and motivating people, as well as in working with colleagues and supervising assistants. This includes a cross-cultural dimension: being a part of centers that focus on international relations and Africa, and teaching African politics, I have had many opportunities to interact with African and other foreign officials and scholars, and I have taught a number of African students.

I believe, based on a review of Equator's activities in its capabilities report, that I would fit into the company best in either the Import-Export or the Merchant Banking Group, but I would be interested in discussing whatever possibilities you think might be appropriate.

A resume is enclosed. Please let me know if I can provide any further information. As I work at home most of the time, it is easiest to reach me there: the address and phone number are on the resume.

Thank you. I look forward to hearing from you.

Sincerely yours,

Mary Helmsley

In her cover letter, Mary elaborates on the relevance of her training and substantive expertise for work at Equator Holdings, as well as on the transferability of her skills from teaching and academic administration. She is able to do this naturally and convincingly because of her basic research into the company. Her second-paragraph reference to her earlier connection with Mr. Holt is effective.

ROBERT J. SCHEINERMAN
Quincy House, Box 00
Cambridge, MA 02138
(617) 493-9876

education

	HARVARD UNIVERSITY CAMBRIDGE, MA
1991	Participant in Business Management Study Group

1986-1989 Master of Arts in Economics, 1989
Special fields in Econometrics, Labor Economics, Macro- and Microeconomics

1982-1986 **BROWN UNIVERSITY** PROVIDENCE, RI
Bachelor of Science, *magna cum laude*, in Applied Mathematics-Economics, 1986
Senior thesis accepted with honors; inducted *Sigma Xi* (scientific honor society).
One of eight members of Student Activities Board which set policies for 125
student organizations.

SOCIETY OF ACTUARIES' EXAMINATIONS
Passed Course Examinations 100 and 110.
Plan to sit for Course Examinations 120, 130, 140 and 150 in Spring 1992.

experience

HARVARD UNIVERSITY CAMBRIDGE, MA
1990-present **Teaching Consultant,** the Derek Bok Center for Teaching and Learning
Counseled graduate student teaching fellows on presentation techniques and
teacher effectiveness. Selected on basis of high student evaluations as a teacher.
1990-present **Assistant Head Tutor,** Economics Department
Hired as one of eight official academic advisers to 500 undergraduate
economics concentrators. Authorized to approve plans of study and course
changes.
1990-present **Resident Tutor,** Quincy House
Advised 40 economics students in undergraduate dormitory. Co-developed
Quincy House economics thesis advising program. Created job of liaison
between house staff and undergraduate students. Hired on basis of superior
performance as a non-resident tutor.
1987-1991 **Teaching Fellow,** Economics Department
Taught weekly sections of courses in American Economic Policy, Intermediate
Macro- and Microeconomics, and Economic Statistics. Wrote exam questions,
met with students, and graded exams. One of ten economics teaching fellows
awarded *Harvard University Certificate of Distinction in Teaching* for 1989-
1990.

1990-1991 **NATIONAL BUREAU OF ECONOMIC RESEARCH** CAMBRIDGE, MA
Research Assistant to Professor Jerry Green
• Conducted data analysis for a project to determine the potential supply of
university professors, using data on Harvard graduates, classes of 1985 to 1990.
• Determined that there had been a marked increase in humanities and life
science concentrators planning academic careers.

1988-1989 **EXECUTIVE OFFICE OF THE PRESIDENT**
COUNCIL OF ECONOMIC ADVISERS WASHINGTON, DC
Junior Staff Economist. The Council of Economic Advisers, the primary
economic advisory board to the President of the United States, consists of 3
appointed members, 10 senior staff economists, and 7 junior staff economists.
• Analyzed economic conditions for Presidents Bush and Reagan, focusing on
GNP growth, inflation, and unemployment
• Researched and edited chapter on free markets and growth in 1989 *Economic
Report of the President.*
• Represented Administration at meetings on trade policy, education, and
statistics improvement.
• Produced background information for and helped write White House
economic briefing memos.
• Ensured economic accuracy of President's speeches.

personal Computer skills: Lotus 1-2-3, Microsoft Excel, Stata, SAS, various graphics
packages. Enjoy skiing on snow and water, swimming, and theater.

Quincy House, Box 00
Cambridge, MA 02138
September 22, 1991

Matthew R. Yarr
State Street Research
Boston, MA 02111

Dear Mr. Yarr:

I would like to meet with you to discuss opportunities in financial services
and securities analysis. I obtained your name from the Career Advisory File
at Harvard, but I wanted to speak to you because of your comments in the
article "Discovery: An Alternate Route to the Boardroom?" in the January-
February 1985 edition of *Harvard Magazine*. I am thrilled at the idea that
the research skills and the patience necessary to succeed in graduate school
can be transferred to a business setting.

At your suggestion, I read Peter Lynch's *One Up on Wall Street* last week.
The book was wonderful in its appeal to simplicity and logic—stick to what
you know. I particularly enjoyed Mr. Lynch's criticisms of my chosen field,
economics. The main problem, as Mr. Lynch described and as I learned from
my experience with the Council of Economic Advisers, is that economics
fails when it is needed most—at the turning points. It is true, however, that
when one remains within the confines of economic logic, there is little
likelihood of developing successful economic forecasting or a get-rich
formula. The field demands the same acuity as that demanded of the
investor, which you describe as "the ability to suspend judgment until the
facts are in, to make your ideas flow from the facts, and not to allow precon-
ceived ideas to color your perceptions of the facts."

I look forward to the opportunity to talk with you, in person or on the phone.
I will call you next week to see if there is a time when we may speak. I have
enclosed my resume for your review.

Thank you very much for your time and assistance.

Sincerely,

Robert J. Scheinerman

Quincy House, Box 00
Cambridge, MA 02138
October 30, 1991

Matthew Yarr
State Street Research
Boston, MA 02111

Dear Matthew:

I appreciate your taking the time to speak with me this morning. Your candid advice was quite helpful.

As you know, I am applying to be a candidate for the Chartered Financial Analyst program. The representative at the ICFA informed me that students can become candidates if they plan to enter a career in financial analysis. It is only necessary to meet the basic requirements, having at least a bachelor's degree and three appropriate letters of reference. Thank you for agreeing to be one of my references. Please fill out the enclosed form and return it to me in the enclosed envelope at your earliest convenience.

Thank you very much for your time and consideration.

Sincerely,

Robert J. Scheinerman

Rob's resume is included as a replica of the Harvard Business School model, including the dates in the margin and lower-case headings. Despite the stated preference against dates in the margin, this format does make you look more like the M.B.A.'s that many businesses routinely hire. Skills and interests get collapsed into the personal section. The type is almost too small, even in the original.

Rob also provides several cover letters. The first, requesting an informational interview from a Career Adviser, brought him kudos because he had done some homework on the person beforehand. His thank-you note (above) is self-explanatory. Notice how in the third letter, a "cold-call" inquiry about employment using the name of another networking contact, he changes the focus to highlight his public policy interests and experience. The fourth and sixth letters make "cold-call" inquiries about actuarial training and/or employment opportunities; the last one to Mercer—in which he elaborates a little on his qualifications and interest in the company, promising a phone follow-up—ultimately produced a job.

Quincy House, Box 00
Cambridge, MA 02138
October 8, 1991

Robert Wilson
Deputy Comptroller
State of Connecticut
55 Elm Street
Hartford, CT

Dear Mr. Wilson:

I am writing to you on the recommendation of David Walsh. We agreed that
I could be of assistance to you with your project on health care costs in Connecticut.

As a graduate student in economics at Harvard, I specialized in labor
economics and econometrics, which have given me a strong background in
applied studies. This training served me well while I was a Junior Staff
Economist on the Council of Economic Advisers (CEA) during 1988-1989.
My primary duties at the CEA were to provide economic analyses of GNP
growth, unemployment levels, and minimum wage effects. This piqued my
interest in public policy, and, after returning to Harvard, I became a teaching
fellow for Professor Martin Feldstein in his course "American Economic
Policy."

Recently, I have taken an interest in studying health economics. During the
past two years, I have attended several related seminars in the economics
department and at the Kennedy School of Government. The topics included
cost containment and comparative health care systems (focusing on the
United States, Canada, and the United Kingdom). My initial interest in the
health care system arose when I worked as an orderly during the summers of
1982 and 1988. The inside view of hospital care was enlightening and
enjoyable.

I look forward to speaking with you to explore how I may be of service to
you. Thank you for your time and consideration.

Sincerely,

Robert J. Scheinerman

enclosure

Quincy House, Box 00
Cambridge, MA 02138
November 18, 1991

Mark Dunster
Keyport Life Insurance Co.
99 High Street, 23rd Floor
Boston, MA 02110

Dear Mr. Dunster:

I am writing to you to apply for a position in the actuarial training program at Keyport Life Insurance Company. Due to my present teaching and advising obligations at Harvard, I would be interested in beginning this summer. After reading the *1992 Associateship Catalog*, I am planning to sit for Course Exams 120, 130, 140, and 150 this spring. The material in these exams overlaps considerably with my graduate and undergraduate training, making this 80-credit load manageable. I have already passed Course Exams 100 and 110.

While at Brown University, I worked as an actuarial at Aetna Life and Casualty for two summers. During the summer of 1985, I worked in the Pension consulting division. My responsibilities included reviewing pension plan modifications and designing spreadsheets for clients to conduct their own sensitivity analyses. The previous summer, I worked in the Corporate Actuarial department, where I analyzed the Life Company general account asset-liability mismatch risk. My other major responsibility was to update the *Life Company Statutory Reserve Catalog*.

Rather than begin my career immediately after college, I accepted admission to Harvard's graduate program in economics. This led to several great opportunities, such as working for the President's Council of Economic Advisers and teaching at Harvard. Furthermore, studying labor economics and econometrics has strengthened my insight into the analysis of employee benefits and demographics, which will enable me to make contributions quickly.

My resume is enclosed for your review. I will call you next week so we may arrange an interview at your convenience. Thank you for your kind consideration.

Sincerely,

Robert J. Scheinerman

Quincy House, Box 00
Cambridge, MA 02138
January 4, 1992

Mark Dunster
Keyport Life Insurance Co.
99 High Street, 23rd Floor
Boston, MA 02110

Dear Mark:

Thank you for giving me the opportunity to visit Keyport Life and to discuss how I might be able to contribute. While the day may have been a bit longer than planned, I was surprised how quickly the time passed. Please let me know if I can provide any additional information.

After our several phone conversations, I was glad to meet you yesterday. I certainly hope we get the chance to work together. Regardless, I hope we will have other chances to meet.

Once again, thanks for your time and consideration.

Sincerely,

Robert J. Scheinerman

Quincy House, Box 00
Cambridge, MA 02138
November 12, 1991

Eliza Belden
Manager, Human Resources
William M. Mercer, Inc.
200 Claredon Street
Boston, MA 02116

Dear Eliza:

I enjoyed speaking with you this morning about opportunities at William M. Mercer, Inc. Mercer sounds like an exciting place to work, allowing its employees much freedom to grow and to succeed. Since I have been out of college for a few years, I am anxious to begin my career at a place where I will be challenged from the first day.

As indicated by the enclosed resume, I have a Master of Arts in economics from Harvard University and have passed the first two actuarial exams. My plans for a heavy exam load in May is due to the significant overlap between my courses at Brown and Harvard and the exam material. In addition to my formal training, my work experience at the Council of Economic Advisers (CEA) and at Harvard would increase my value to Mercer.

The CEA is the primary group responsible for economic advising to the President. Since it consists of only 20 economists, each must be able to work quickly, accurately, and independently. There is little forgiveness for tardiness or mistakes at the White House. At Harvard, I have worked as a teaching fellow, a research assistant, and an adviser. Teaching has been particularly rewarding since it allowed me the chance to share my training with the students, while strengthening my presentation skills.

I will call you next week to arrange an interview so we can explore further how I can contribute at Mercer. Thank you for your time and consideration.

Sincerely,

Robert J. Scheinerman

Joseph Clark
00 Harvard Rd.
Cambridge, MA 02138
617-666-6666

Education:
Harvard University, Cambridge MA
Post-Doctoral Fellow in Biology (Molecular Biology), 1991-present.
Duke University, Durham NC
Ph.D., Biological Sciences (Cell and Developmental Biology), 1991.
M.A., Liberal Studies (Concentration in the Sciences), 1985.
Columbia University, New York NY
B.S., Major in Biology, 1983.

Research Experience:
Harvard University, Department of Genetics.
Post-Doctoral Fellow (1991-present). Current projects include investigating how gene expression is regulated and integrated between the two
distinct genetic systems of chloroplast and nucleus using mutants and
transgenics, and the isolation of chloroplast RNA polymerase(s) that
transcribe different types of plastid gene promoters in Chlamydomonas.
Research Assistant (1989-1991). Studied the regulation of plastid gene
promoters in transgenic chloroplasts and the *in vivo* expression of
foreign chimeric genes.
Duke University, Department of Biological Sciences.
Graduate Student (1985-1991). Thesis Title: Developmental expression
of storage proteins in soybean. Analyzed the developmental, biochemi-
cal and molecular expression of storage proteins found in different
tissues and cells of soybean, Glycine max, including purification,
characterization and molecular cloning studies of developmentally
expressed storage proteins.

Teaching Experience:
Harvard University
Teaching Fellow, Dept. of Biochemistry and Molecular Biology (Spring
1992). Basic Principles of Biochemistry and Cell Biology: Instructed
laboratory principles and techniques of protein biochemistry and
enzymology.
Teaching Fellow, Department of Cellular and Developmental Biology
(Spring 1991). Cell Biology: Created and directed a laboratory research
project on the molecular biology of chloroplast transformation.
Duke University
Teaching Assistant (1984-89). Planned and prepared laboratory lectures
and experiments and led and organized discussion sections for courses
such as Molecular Biology of Prokaryotes and Lower Ekaryotes,
Organization and Development of Plants, Plant Physiology, Genetics
and Introductory Biology.
Marshfield Academy (Bloomfield, NJ)
Science Instructor (1983-85). Taught college preparatory courses in
Biology, Introductory Chemistry/Physics; Head Housemaster; Head
Varsity Lacrosse Coach (State Champions 1983, 1984); Wilderness
Experience Leader.

Joe was seeking to move into patent law, a career where scientific expertise is crucial.
Thus he emphasizes his education and research experience and skills. He appended
a page listing his publications (not included here).

March 9, 1992

Dr. Kathleen Martin
Metcalf & Tucker
Suite 2500
One Financial Center
Boston, Massachusetts 02111

Dear Dr. Martin:

Your comments during last week's OCS panel on "Alternatives to Bench Careers for a Scientist" offered me a glimpse of the contributions a scientist makes to the patenting process. Unfortunately, after the panel time was too short to continue an in-depth conversation with you regarding patent law as a career path for a molecular biologist.

On this note, I would appreciate the opportunity to learn more about your thoughts and perspectives on the patent business and the specifics of the profession.

I will call you later in the week to see if I can arrange a meeting at your convenience. Thank you.

Sincerely,

Joseph Clark, Ph.D.
Postdoctoral Fellow in Biology

Joe provides several cover letters he wrote during the course of his search, the first requesting an informational interview, the second to request an interview with the senior partner heading the patent law group at the same law firm, and the third a thank-you letter to that partner. The letters seem self-explanatory and have, along with his conscientious research and preparation for interviews, ultimately garnered Joe a job at a premier law firm.

April 13, 1992

Mr. Paul T. Tucker
Metcalf & Tucker
Suite 2500
One Financial Center
Boston, Massachusetts 02110

Dear Mr. Tucker:

I am contacting you and Mr. John M. Welch to express an interest in joining the biotechnology patent group at Metcalf & Tucker. A Harvard career panel and meeting with Dr. Kathleen Martin have acquainted me with the firm.

Although not yet a patent agent, I intend to study for the patent bar exam and aspire to attend law school in Boston. Patent law attracts me because it offers an inherent opportunity for diverse intellectual challenges and works to effect positive results for inventors.

As a postdoctoral fellow and graduate student I have pursued a course of study and research in molecular and cell biology. My decision to enter this field was made while teaching at Marshfield Academy and concurrently studying for the Master's in Liberal Studies at Duke. Teaching attracted me to research. Moreover, the Liberal Studies program provided for advanced interdisciplinary investigation focusing on issues in science and technology, ranging from course work in ethics to the politics of the nuclear age.

Molecular biology is undergoing rapid expansion, fueled no doubt by advances in technology and the realization that significant economic reward can be gained by manipulating living organisms and their molecules in novel ways. Participation in the research process has afforded me a window to the conceptual and analytical tools that are the foundation for such innovation.

I would welcome the opportunity to meet with you and your colleagues to discuss my background, qualifications and how my talents might be useful to Metcalf & Tucker and the scientific community it represents.

Sincerely,

Joseph Clark, Ph.D.
Postdoctoral Fellow in Biology

June 3, 1992

Mr. Paul Tucker
Metcalf & Tucker
Suite 2500
One Financial Center
Boston, Massachusetts 02110

Dear Mr. Tucker:

Thank you very much for meeting with me and introducing me to your colleagues. I enjoyed talking with you, as well as with others in the biotech group, and found our conversation to be both interesting and profitable.

I also learned a great deal from the others about the biotech group, the demands of the profession and their legal careers. Everyone was helpful and informative; moreover, I especially liked the atmosphere of your firm. It is most impressive.

For your information, I have enclosed a copy of my resume and a reprint of a recent PNAS paper on which I am co-author. If you have any further questions, please do not hesitate to call.

Again, thank you very much for your time and consideration. Best wishes for an enjoyable and productive summer.

Sincerely,

Joseph Clark

00 Martindale St., Apt. 0
Cambridge, MA 02138
Tel.: 822-0000
March 22, 1991

Maureen Johnson
David R. Godine, Publisher
300 Mass Ave.
Boston, MA 02115

Dear Ms. Johnson:

You may recall our telephone conversation yesterday afternoon, when you kindly encouraged me to apply for a part-time internship position with David R. Godine. As I mentioned to you, I am currently completing my doctorate for the Comparative Literature Dept. at Harvard University. I plan to remain at Harvard next year as a Lecturer in the History and Literature Concentration, to recast my dissertation but also to explore nonacademic career options, especially in the realm of publishing. The summer months of June, July and August are those I have set aside to initiate this research through a suitable internship.

At a recent panel discussion at the Harvard Office of Career Services, your internship was cited as the best for graduate students interested in the editorial side of publishing. Your own description of the varied tasks and texts involved have further convinced me that such an internship is ideally suited to my aims of exploring the field while acquiring hands-on experience. (I might add that I am not deterred by the thought of 'busy-work' or clerical duties.)

Beyond my prolonged training as a reader, critic and teacher of literature, I would also tell you about myself that I am a native speaker of French (who has spent many years in France), with fluent Spanish, a good reading knowledge of Russian, and an acquaintance with Italian and German. I have always been motivated by a strong curiosity to delve into different cultures and intellectual disciplines. At this point, I am extremely eager to develop skills that might allow me to extend and apply my academic background in new ways.

I have enclosed my c.v.; my academic dossier is available upon request. I would like to thank you for talking with me the other day and look forward to hearing from you.

Sincerely yours,

Catherine Fuller

This strong cover letter (resume is not reproduced here) followed a semi-"cold" telephone inquiry and yielded an internship in publishing for Catherine. Note that she created a slight "in" by referring to an OCS panel presentation at which the company was represented.

Chapter 5

৵

Mounting the Job Search and Getting the Job Offer

In practice, there is usually no clear line between mounting the actual job search and all the previous steps. You have undoubtedly been "searching" all along. But let's assume that you are now ready to search in earnest. How do you prepare yourself for the shortest, most enjoyable ordeal possible?

Preliminaries

Prepare psychologically. This advice is, of course, easier to give than to take. But it's worth taking! *The trick is to achieve **and maintain** an optimistic, self-confident, and, at the same time, realistic attitude.* Try to view the search as an adventure and enjoy the learning process. Keep firmly in mind that you are engaged in a matching process: you are looking for the right job as much as employers are seeking the right employee. In the spirit of realism, prepare for a long search (four to eight months or longer in a recession or when changing careers), apply for many jobs, and be incredibly persistent—or "politely relentless," as one Career Adviser put it. Assertiveness is crucial in this process; but, at the same time, be friendly and considerate to everyone you contact, from the secretaries on up.

Prepare for rejection, which is virtually inevitable in a job search, in likely contrast to your academic experience. Do not take it personally—it's very important to maintain self-confidence—but also try to seek out and respond to feedback that might improve your chances. Finally, be flexible and open-minded, even while holding out for your basic values and essential job requirements. Put another way, stay open to the role of serendipity in careers; GSAS alumni recount wonderful stories of unexpected twists of fate that led them into unplanned career directions. For example, Nancy Pyle, who was finishing up her dissertation on Muslim art and architecture in Turkey, was encouraged to apply for a job administering the Kennedy School of Government's Mason Fellows Program by an acquaintance she happened to sit next to at a dinner party. She would never have heard of or thought about this job of recruiting, admitting, and supervising government officers from developing countries in a one-year M.P.A. program, but decided to apply almost as a lark. Fortunately for her, no one bothered to inform her that the job description specified an economist. In fact, she got the job, which launched a highly successful career at the Harvard Institute for International Development, which in turn led to a job as President Bok's assistant for developing international programs at the University and, most recently, to the position as Vice President for Planning and Development of The American University in Beirut.

Create a structure. First, the practicalities. Unlike the highly structured academic job market, the nonacademic market requires you to create the structure. Think of your search as a half- to full-time job and structure your days and weeks accordingly with job-search activities. Set *realistic* daily, weekly, and monthly goals for yourself, and write them down, adjusting them as necessary. For example, plan to make a certain number of calls, write a specified number of letters, and read the ads each day. (Refer to the sample schedule at the end of this chapter.) Continue to keep excellent, up-to-date records. An appointment calendar devoted solely to the job search is a helpful tool, as well as the usual filing system (cards, notebooks, accordion folders, computer files—whatever serves you best). You might want to organize an informal support group of friends in like circumstances (or not) to keep you on the track and buoyed up.

Other preparation. Make sure your resume is in order and line up your references, if you haven't already done so. Buy an answering machine and record a professional message (no background music or clever jokes). Review and continue to revise your self-assessment and exploration notes. Ask friends and acquaintances about their experiences and for advice from their job searches. Continue to do "market research" on industries, companies/organizations, job descriptions, typical salaries and benefits, etc. (See the Bibliography for sources.)

Rob Scheinerman, an A.B.D. in Economics whose resume you encountered in Chapter 4, decided over a period of several months of self-assessment, informational interviewing, and research that he wanted to pursue a nonacademic career as an actuary (after eliminating investment banking and management consulting). Two months of intense effort that followed this decision yielded Rob a job offer in a small Boston insurance company. His descriptions of and advice from the process he went through are woven into this section.

Finding Jobs

Generate targets, i.e., job openings or possibilities that will lead to interviews. The first step is to *activate your network*: write or call all your contacts (except OCS Career Advisers, unless they have specifically indicated they will help you) and tell them that you are now actively looking for a specified kind of job and would appreciate their informing you of any job leads. Remind these contacts periodically that you are still looking, perhaps every couple of months. As you've probably heard, a substantial majority of jobs are both found and filled through personal contacts.

Next, continually *peruse advertised job listings*—in the classified sections of newspapers, professional journals, specialized publications[1] and databases, OCS and other career office job binders, job fairs, and outplacement services. Although the expected yield is not high, you might be among the many who find the perfect match this way.

Consider utilizing an increasingly popular source of networking contacts and job possibilities—*electronic bulletin boards*. Go beyond the new resume distribution and job-listing services to the large national bulletin boards such as *Compuserve* or *Prodigy* and especially to the

---

1. Examples include: *Community Jobs, Non Profit Times, Federal Jobs Digest, International Employment Opportunities, Chronicle of Higher Education, Art Search.*

thousands of smaller and often specialized boards, where job needs and leads are regularly exchanged. *Write letters to executives with the capacity to hire in targeted organizations*—if possible, to people referred by one of your contacts. Also look for people with advanced degrees in high-level positions, who are more likely to respond to a "cold-call" letter. These letters will be somewhat more general than the cover letter responding to a specific job listing and must have an extra zip and appeal. You might try approaching these people with an idea for a position or special project and persuade them to talk to you (and ultimately, you hope, to hire you). Follow up your letters with a phone call and try to get an interview, even if there is no current job opening. This targeted cold-call approach is an especially appropriate strategy when you are limited to a particular geographic area. It is encouraging that 81 percent of the respondents in a survey of Fortune 1000 companies claimed that they had hired someone who had sent them an unsolicited letter.[2]

If you are feeling confident, you could try "cold" telephone calls to targeted people. You must first get through the secretary barrier and then present your goal, reasons for changing fields, essential qualifications, and sales pitch, as well as request an interview to explore options and get advice—and you need to do this all within about five minutes and in a manner that balances chutzpah with courtesy. If you choose this approach, be sure to prepare an informal "script" beforehand, and to follow up with a resume and a cover letter that repeats the request in writing and (if you're lucky) confirms the appointment.

Most job-search manuals warn you to avoid human resources (or personnel) offices like the plague. In general, you do want to go right to the person with the capacity to hire you directly or indirectly, who may well have more flexible criteria than a human resources officer. But many companies and organizations insist on routing you through human resources (and many have improved the quality of their personnel functions accordingly), so you should be prepared to work with and impress personnel staff. Even when they play a relatively minor role, enlisting them as allies can make a crucial difference. (This is also true of secretaries and any other "gatekeepers.") Technical consulting or research organizations will have technically trained personnel staff, often

2. Half, *Robert Half on Hiring*, 221.

with advanced degrees in the relevant fields. If you must start with a personnel officer or recruiter, try to find an experienced one, who will probably have more imagination and perspective, and hence a greater appreciation of graduate training.

> After this decision [to become an actuary] I called the Society of Actuaries to find out about training programs at companies and about the accreditation process. . . . Since I wanted to stay in Boston (my wife is a student), I wrote to every firm in Boston (insurance companies and consulting firms) which had a program I wanted to enter. In each letter I suggested a date when I would call to arrange an interview. Since many national consulting firms did not list a Boston office, I called their headquarters and asked if they did hire at my level in Boston. This added four more companies to my list.[3]
>
> — *Rob Scheinerman*

Finally, look for recruiting programs appropriate for or even geared to graduate students, for example, those at OCS and, for scientists, at M.I.T. (Harvard graduate students may use the M.I.T. Career Services Office and may even participate in their recruiting programs, subject to certain restrictions.) Some students inquire about using headhunters. Although headhunters occasionally list jobs at OCS and some specialize in relevant areas (e.g., bilingual Japanese jobs or technical jobs), they are typically recruiting for higher-level management positions for which most of you would not qualify. If all else fails, look for interim freelance, consulting, or other bridging jobs.

> Once I determined a career and a region, I started to find out about what typical offers included. This meant learning about work responsibilities, salaries, vacations, support for accreditation as an actuary, promotion timing and bonuses . . .
>
> *Take rejection in stride.* By Thanksgiving I already had two letters which expressed apologies. Several more came in December. Often I had already spoken to the recruiter. Even after these letters came, I called companies periodically to see if their hiring positions had changed or when they expected openings. Whenever I called I asked if would be okay for me to check

3. Rob Scheinerman, letter to the author, June 5, 1992.

back in a month. This way I might not seem like a major pest. *Even if no openings exist, try to get an information interview.* One partner at a consulting firm was willing to speak with me for an hour, and arranged for me to meet with a recently hired employee. Although no formal interview followed, I put myself in a position of being a known quantity should an opening occur. I also learned that this company was not for me. *Never feel desperate.* Even with most companies expressing regrets, I continued to call those who did not yet respond. With each call, I was positive and upbeat. One key: Never give them a chance to say NO. Persistence on the phone with one company got me to the top of their resume list. In early January I had an interview and by mid-January I had an offer.[4]

— Rob Scheinerman

Creating Your Own Job

If you feel bold, creative, and somewhat entrepreneurial, consider the unusual but often successful job-search strategy of creating your own job and selling it to an established employer. Simply put, this generally requires diagnosing an employer's need and figuring out what you can do to meet it.

Eighteen years ago, Tressa Ruslander Miller, whose training was in fine arts, approached Security Pacific Corporation and persuaded them to hire her to establish a visual and performing arts program for its new downtown Los Angeles corporate headquarters. Not just like that, of course: First, she figured out that the bank needed to make its headquarters building a point of destination for customers not used to coming downtown, a more stimulating place for its employees, and a force in creating a business partnership with the established civic community. She approached an executive in the marketing department, for whom she had researched an artwork for his personal collection, and he told her that there was no job, only corporate pressure to do something with the vast lobby and outdoor plaza space, and invited her to make a proposal to solve the problem. With his blessing, Tressa proceeded to survey the bank employees and interview top management and community leaders, and

4. Rob Scheinerman, letter to the author, June 5, 1992.

eventually proposed an ongoing series of high-quality musical, visual arts, and cultural events.

The bank agreed and thus Tressa began a highly successful career at Security Pacific in the nascent field of arts administration (it's always easier to break in cold to a new field, she says). The job evolved into a focus on visual art exhibitions showcasing young California artists, increasing liaison with the larger arts community, and an expanding role in acquiring and managing the bank's considerable art collection. Following the bank's recent merger with Bank of America, Tressa has started her own business, Fine Arts Consulting.[5]

Long-Distance Job Searches[6]

Those of you who are conducting long-distance job searches will need to be especially imaginative and persistent in creating a long-distance network. If you know exactly where you want to be and can manage it, you should plan to move first and conduct an "on-site" search. The following suggestions will facilitate an on-site search but are aimed primarily at those of you with multiple location options and/or constraints on leaving your present home before you have a job.

1. Research locations that offer good opportunities in your field. Do this by talking to everyone you know with connections to or special information about various locations. Check out sources such as the *Places Rated Almanac* and *Fortune*'s "Ten Best Cities to Work In" (which comes out annually in the late fall). Also write to chambers of commerce in potential locations and ask for their materials, including maps.

2. Buy the local newspaper(s) for the places you are considering—especially the Sunday paper. (The Out of Town Newsstand in Harvard Square can order newspapers if it doesn't already carry them.) Read the paper to get a general sense of the place and for specific news with implications for job openings, as well as information from the want ads and real estate sections on available jobs, prevailing wages, and the cost of housing.

5. See also the account in *Kissing the Dragon* (Cosman, Chapter 13) of creating a job from scratch.
6. Thanks to Judy Kugel, Director of the Career Services Office at the Kennedy School of Government, Harvard University, for her material on the long-distance search.

3. Start to build a network in the targeted location(s). Question all your friends and family, former and current colleagues, receptive professors, acquaintances from all corners of your life (e.g., church or temple, outside activities, high school, college, and graduate school), and professional people you know (dentists, bankers, lawyers, etc.) for the names of contacts. This should yield a small nucleus of people in the targeted areas to get you started on information interviews and further networking. Take advantage of OCS's Career Advisory Service geographical file and the listing of local Harvard Clubs. Seek out, contact, and consider joining the appropriate local chapter of the national professional association(s) for your new field. Attend and network at national professional conferences, if possible.

In general, it is advisable to precede phone contact with an introductory letter, saying that you are planning to relocate (not simply thinking of it) and requesting their assistance in assessing the job market and providing further contacts.

4. Meanwhile, consult relevant directories, using the geographical indexes, and look at the *JobBank* series (published for 18 cities) and the various field-specific periodicals that list jobs, in addition to the local papers.

5. You will have to use the telephone for information interviews, networking, and even job-screening interviews, so polish your introductory "pitch" and try to enlist the help of the "gatekeepers" in getting you through to the person you want to speak with. (Sometimes you can reach that person directly before and after regular business hours, after the staff has left.) Keep time zone differences in mind and use them to your advantage whenever possible. Work on your telephone manner and always be prepared for a full-fledged encounter when you place the call. And, of course, be persistent in following up on letters and phone calls.

6. Determine in advance under what conditions you would be willing to travel for an on-site job interview, probably at your own expense. Don't let graduate student penury prevent you from taking advantage of an excellent job possibility.

The Interview

As you can imagine or know from experience, an invitation to a job interview presents you with both a crucial hurdle *and* an opportunity. In one or two visits you must convince the employer/interviewer that you are the best and safest person for the job, or if not the safest, at least one for whom the potential benefits outweigh the risks. This requires you to describe and present yourself in a self-serving but non-bragging way. *Therefore, you must be self-aware, controlled, and highly prepared while appearing to be relaxed and genuine, even spontaneous!*

It reduces the pressure on you to remember that the interview also affords *you* the opportunity to evaluate *them.* Think of it as a *mutual exploration of fit.* Those who lack experience and/or confidence in their interviewing skills might find the detailed explication of the process given here useful.

Interview preparation. PREPARE, PREPARE, PREPARE! If you have done your self-assessment and career exploration thoroughly, you need only focus that knowledge on the particular job for which you are interviewing. Consider the following:

1. *Who are you?* What skills, strengths, and relevant background do you bring to this job and organization? Think of your potential liabilities or deficits and prepare to disarm the interviewer. Do you have any strikes against you in their eyes (age, gender, etc.)? For example, how will you handle stereotypes about academics or doubts about the relevance of your experience and skills? It may reassure you to know that several alumni reported great success once they got the interview, precisely because they could counter the stereotypes more effectively in person. For example, the man who interviewed Ellen Glew (Ph.D., German) at Wang told her: "There has to be a job here for a person like you and I'm going to find it!" [7]

2. *Also consider the image you want to project.* It will, of course, depend on the job and company, because you want to project yourself as the solution to their hiring problem. At the same time, consider the following general qualities as ones you might want to communicate (while maintaining your integrity):

---

7. Personal communication with the author.

- high competence generally and in areas needed
- breadth and flexibility, adaptability: best athlete, not best basketball player
- results, achievement orientation
- team player, congenial, easy to work with
- communication abilities
- high motivation, commitment, energy
- originality, imagination
- honesty, trustworthiness
- specific characteristics, expertise, and skills required

3. *Who are they?* What is *their* "hiring problem"? What is the job they want done—both the explicit, advertised job and the implicit potential job (i.e., what you can make of it, which they may not have articulated). Find out as much as you can about the company and job from the usual sources: information interviews, company materials such as annual reports and client brochures (get them ahead of time), *Lotus One Source*, periodical and trade literature, the job announcement, and inside sources (if you should be so lucky!). Learn the vocabulary, if you haven't already. Investigate related and/or competitive groups and organizations. Find out what typical job offers look like, if possible. Incidentally, the most frequently voiced complaint of Harvard recruiters and Fortune 1000 interviewers is that job candidates don't know enough about their companies.[8]

4. *Anticipate questions.* Put yourself in their shoes and write out questions you would ask yourself. Remember, they want to ascertain how you will perform in this job at their organization over time. The questions are likely to fall into the following types:

- Ascertaining skills and personal qualities such as character and motivation that are related to the job: e.g., Tell me about yourself. What are your greatest strengths and weaknesses? Why do you want this job? Why should we hire you above other qualified applicants?
- Eliciting past experience and achievements that bear on future performance: e.g., What major problem have you encountered (or an experience where you had difficulties with a boss or coworker) and how did you deal with it? What is your management (or work) style? What did you like most and least about your last job? Why did you leave your last job?

8. Half, *Robert Half on Hiring*, 227.

• Ascertaining your knowledge of the job, company, profession, and whether your career goals are realistic: e.g., Why do you want to work for us? What do you see yourself doing five years from now? What do you know about our organization/company? Are you willing to travel/relocate?

• Posing hypothetical cases to "test" your ability to analyze a situation or solve a problem on your feet (this is particularly common for consulting and investment banking job interviews): e.g., How would you estimate how many tombstones are sold in the U.S. each year? How would you solve this (specified) problem of ours?

• Questioning your motivation and qualifications for the career change: e.g., Why are you making this change? How can we be sure you won't return to academia if you have the chance? How will you deal with starting at the bottom, with younger colleagues? We believe that you are "overqualified"/"underqualified" for this position.

5. *Think out and jot down your answers to these anticipated questions.* Try to allay their presumed fears or concerns and convey your enthusiasm for this job and organization. For example, in response to an open-ended question such as "Tell me about yourself," reveal—concisely—the aspects of yourself and your past experience that relate to the job. Or, in response to a question regarding your accomplishments, give an example that shows your ability to operate in an environment like theirs, such as experience in meeting deadlines or accomplishing goals in a team setting.

Judy Esterquest (now Director of Professional Development at Booz-Allen, whose career development is described at the end of Chapter 2) recommends preparing "road-tested modules of explanation" of your academic discipline and scholarly interests (or thesis) to make them seem interesting, worthwhile, and relevant to the nonacademic world. She relates an experience during an interview when a skeptical corporate executive confronted her: "So your thesis was about Hamlet, eh? I've always hated Hamlet; he's such a wimp, takes five acts to exact his revenge!" Whereupon Judy replied, "Well, I certainly understand your point. But you've got to understand that Shakespeare was fundamentally a businessman." "Oh, how so?" "Well, you see, he had to have Hamlet procrastinate for those five acts; otherwise, nobody would've paid for admission!"[9] She apparently captivated her critic.

9. Personal communication with the author.

This story raises another point, namely, the *power of anecdotes in interviews*. Think of compelling, unusual, or humorous *stories* to illustrate your experiences or qualities. They will stick in the interviewer's mind long after most of what you have said has faded from memory. You also need to anticipate *inappropriate or illegal questions*: about marital status, pregnancy, age, race and ethnicity, religion, and disabilities. You may choose to volunteer information that will allay the underlying, unspoken concern. For example, if you have a disability, consider explaining how you will deal with it so that it doesn't impinge on your job performance. Or you may want to politely and matter-of-factly ask the interviewer to explain how this information is relevant to the job. If the question is an egregious violation, you may decide to terminate the interview at that point and even to report it to the Equal Employment Opportunity Commission.

Also prepare questions to ask them about aspects of the job or organization that are still unclear and about the process (e.g., when can I expect to hear from you?). It is considered bad form (i.e., premature) to ask about salary or benefit particulars at this stage. Try to get a better sense of the potential, challenges, and pitfalls of this job and organization, as well as how well it fits *your* needs. (Review your list of characteristics a job must and must not have.) Demonstrate your sophistication and preparation with your questions.

6. Consider doing a *videotaped mock interview* at OCS.

7. *Work on your mental set*. You have much to offer them. They are after a match too. They want you to do well so they can fill the position and get on with their work, and you are more likely to establish that intangible but critical rapport with the interviewer if you are confident and engaged.

The interview proper. We'll begin with some **practical tips**:

1. *Dress* will depend somewhat on the profession and the organization, but in general, dress professionally, comfortably, and neatly, and err (if at all) on the conservative side. Women should avoid clothes that might cause them to worry about how much they are exposing. Layered clothing protects you from unexpected temperature conditions. Don't ignore or overdo other obvious elements of self-presentation, such as hair, make-up, or deodorant/perfume.

2. *Bring along extra resumes and any other relevant materials,* such as portfolios or writing samples.

3. *Be on time.* If possible, check out the location ahead of time. Allow extra time for unforeseen contingencies. If—heaven forbid!—you are going to be late, call ahead.

4. *Take a few minutes* before the interview to take in your surroundings and to get yourself centered and into a confident mindset. Remember to stay engaged in the here-and-now of the interview, and leave the postmortems till later.

Preliminaries. (1) Remember that your *body language* communicates at least as much as your words and tone of voice. So sit comfortably without slumping (avoiding very soft chairs or sofas, if possible) so that you can lean forward to convey interest and enthusiasm. In general, you want to maintain an alert, engaged posture and expression. (2) Plan to maintain reasonable *eye contact.* If that is difficult for you, establish a semblance of eye contact by looking at the spot between the eyes. (3) Take your cue on the firmness and length of the *handshake* from the interviewer. For example, meet a limp handshake with a slightly firmer but not a crushing one; never meet a firm handshake with a limp one.

Interview structure. First interviews tend to follow a predictable structure, beginning with a couple of minutes devoted to *small talk.* The main part of the interview consists of the *substance of your self-presentation*, where you *subtly take control of the interview.* Make sure you get across what you want to, including presenting character traits they can't ask you about directly (e.g., integrity, dependability). You want to be conversational but concise. Be prepared to give a 90-second spiel about yourself as you relate to the job, if the interviewer should create the opportunity ("Tell me about yourself"). This is where you employ your "disarming responses" where appropriate—for example, anticipating concerns about your status as an academic. STAY CONFIDENT. For example, *don't be apologetic about graduate school*; rather, present your degree as a positive achievement and as an indicator of future performance. DO NOT LIE OR BLUFF. If you need a little time to consider a response, ask for it. STAY POSITIVE; for example, do not criticize former bosses or thesis advisers or your department.

Homer Hagedorn, whose career has been in organizational development, offers more subtle advice: try to engage sensitively in the process so that you demonstrate to the interviewer that people benefit simply from interacting with you, that "valuable work" occurs wherever and whenever you participate.

Toward the end of the allotted time you will be asked if you have any questions. This is the point where you trot out *your prepared or spontaneous questions* about the job and the company, including when you can expect to hear from them. You might consider (but only if it is comfortable for you in the particular situation) a bold inquiry about whether there is anything at this time that might be standing in the way of your candidacy.[10] If you get a substantive response, you can shape your *closing statement* to it. In any case, you want to close strongly, reiterating your enthusiasm, your strengths, and your match with the job.

Salary questions. In general, you want to avoid discussing salaries until you have an offer. However, an interviewer may well ask you what your salary requirements are. Although you should give some thought to this question in advance, deflect it, if possible, by indicating you want to find out more about the job. If pressed, avoid naming a figure if you can possibly help it; rather, ask what their salary range is or how much they had in mind. If still pressed, give a range which hooks into the top of their range. Avoid giving your past salary as a basis for judgment unless you know that it was slightly or moderately higher than what they offer.

Telephone interviews. Some employers resort to telephone interviews for screening purposes, either to reduce a too-large pool of highly qualified candidates or when geographic distance precludes an in-person interview until the final stages. In addition to the above advice, follow common-sense rules: schedule the interview for a time when you will be fresh and undistracted. Try to imagine a person on the other end of the phone to make the conversation feel more personal so that you can convey warmth and congeniality in your voice.

Stress interviews. Particularly in high-stress career fields or environments, employers may employ "stress interview" tactics in order to screen out applicants who cannot coolly respond to the pressure. Stress interviews are characterized by unnerving or indifferent questions and responses to your answers, often delivered in antagonistic tones, such as: What makes you think you could perform under constant deadline pressure after you've been lazing around at Harvard for the past six years? Why would you waste your time on seventeenth-century British history?

10. This technique was suggested by Neil McKenna of McKenna, Jendl and Associates, Inc.

Could you explain how any particle of your experience relates to what we do? Why should we hire someone so overqualified for this position? The interviewer may also refuse to make eye contact, interrupt frequently, conduct other business, and/or subject you to the silent treatment—waiting for you to nervously leap in and babble revealingly.

Your best course of action is to anticipate and rehearse your responses to these possibilities and keep from getting flustered or angry. In this way you will indicate that you are aware of what's happening and are immune to their games. For example, you could sit silently or you could ask whether there's more information the interviewer wants on a particular issue. Remain polite and pleasant, and consider using humor if it seems appropriate. Maintain your dignity.

Second interviews. Second interviews, *if* they occur, are analogous to campus visits after interviews at the annual meetings for some academic disciplines. You've made it to the short list and thus they have an even greater stake in having you succeed; but you've also got to perform under heavier scrutiny and over a longer period of time. You will likely meet several potential bosses and colleagues, usually serially, and you must fight the "broken record syndrome" by staying fresh, engaged, and enthusiastic even after the eighth interview. At this stage they want to confirm that you can perform well in the job, but also that you will fit in, work well *with* them, and wear well over time. So keep your guard up, especially during social occasions and over lunch or dinner, while still managing to seem relaxed, honest, and "yourself." Remember that you're evaluating them, too, and hang on to your sense of humor. Salary discussions may come up at this stage. Follow the principles discussed above and in Chapter 7 on negotiation.

Post-interview activity. No R and R yet for the weary! You neglect the post-interview tasks at your peril. First, write up the interview immediately. This is your chance to evaluate the experience and come up with any changes for the next one. Make notes about the process and what you've learned about the job and place, including the information you still need in order to decide whether you want the job. Think about aspects you might want to negotiate.

Write a follow-up letter within one to three days, expressing your appreciation, reiterating your enthusiasm (or regretfully indicating that you think this is not a good match after all), and adding any new information or thoughts that might strengthen your case ("Upon further reflection, . . ."). If you need to send receipts for your travel expenses, do so in a separate letter.

Continue to generate other options and interviews. The worst that could happen is that you have a choice. If more than one week has passed and you haven't heard from the organization, then by all means call to inquire about the status of the search. Even if you don't receive any useful information, you can at least convey your continuing interest in the job.

The Job Offer

First, let's deal with how to receive a rejection call or letter. Express regret and leave the door open for future possibilities. If you feel comfortable about it, ask them if they would tell you their reasons for not selecting you; you may get valuable feedback. It is difficult not to take rejection personally, but you must continue to think positively about yourself, use your support system, and keep looking.

Now let's assume that your labors have finally been rewarded and you have a job offer. Understandably, your first impulse might be to accept it immediately, right over the phone. Ignore this impulse, unless you have already gone through the steps discussed below.

A wiser course is to thank the employer (or whoever offers the job), express your pleasure and enthusiasm (and inclination to accept, if it's true), clarify the offer, say you want to think it over, and ask to get back to him or her in a few days or a week or even two weeks. (The employer may have his or her own timetable, to which you would try to accommodate.)

Decision. Is this *really* the job you want? Does it fulfill the conditions you have kept in mind all along (characteristics any job *must* and *must not* have), or is it likely to *lead* to the "right" job? If not, are you making a compromise based on a realistic assessment of the existing job market, or out of fear that a "better" job won't turn up soon? (If dual-career issues are involved, see the next section of this chapter.)

Check out all your other options. Call all preferred employers where you are being considered, even remotely; explain your situation and inquire about the extent of their interest in you. Generate as many alternatives as possible, both to help you feel less desperate and to aid in possible negotiations. In the end, however, you may need to do some heavy soul-searching, without sufficient information, both alone and with close friends and advisers.

Dual-Career Issues

The foregoing has largely assumed an individual exploration, search, and decision-making process, which the prevalence of dual-career couples renders increasingly obsolete. (Dual-career here means that both partners seek a career, in contrast to the case where one partner has a career and the other is primarily a wage-earner or full-time homemaker or volunteer.) In fact, you may well be considering nonacademic careers to gain increased flexibility in a two-career relationship. Dual careers, as you may well have discovered, can be very tricky, stressful, and even painful to manage. These tips for approaching the job search may help get yours started on the right track.[11]

1. Start early with and continue to pay attention to self-assessment, particularly regarding your values. Both as individuals and as a couple, set priorities among your work-related and other central values, especially family. Think about such options as commuter marriage. (Under what conditions, if any? For how long?)

2. Start your career planning and job-search process early and jointly. Strive to think flexibly, broadly, and creatively. More specifically, depending on your field and interests, how flexible can each of you be in type of work (e.g., economists vs. most humanists)? Or in career trajectory (e.g., taking turns focusing intensely on your careers)?

3. Start out listing all the geographic locations where you could or would take a job, ranging from "good enough" to "wonderful." It is important to generate "good enough" possibilities. Look for the points of overlap in your lists. Use the concept of regions, not cities.

4. If one partner is geographically unmovable (is this a joint decision?), think in terms of the regional area, alternative kinds of work, and a different career trajectory. Can you take turns with career primacy or job choices? Is a commuter marriage viable for you?

11. Thanks to Dr. Patricia K. Light, Director of the Harvard Business School Counseling Service, for her contributions to this section.

5. Even if one partner has a strong geographical preference (e.g., an existing job) that the other hopes to honor, that partner should nevertheless start investigating alternatives in the locations of choice for the other *early* on in the process. Otherwise, the couple will face a dilemma at the end.

6. If both of you are starting from scratch at the same time, it's easiest to coordinate searches *if* you start the process early and with flexible attitudes. Be creative with applications and job negotiations (e.g., consider split positions, part-time positions, positions elsewhere in the organization), and use your spouse's contacts to help with your search.

7. When it comes to making a decision, face the issues openly, honestly, and thoroughly. How will you feel about turning this job down? Are you likely to blame your spouse and harbor bitterness and resentment? How would you feel about taking this job at the expense of your spouse's career—selfish? guilty? How will you minimize regret? How would it be to live apart for a transitional period? Have you exhausted all of the alternatives? In these matters, listen to your heart as well as your head.

ORGANIZING YOUR JOB SEARCH

Sample Weekly Calendar

Sunday
1. Read want ads from targeted region newspaper(s).
2. Respond with resume and cover letter to "quality" positions.
3. Review week's calendar and prepare questions for networking sessions.
4. Call 3 friends/relatives/contacts for the names of persons working in the fields you have targeted.
5. Log in to electronic bulletin boards.

Monday
1. Place follow-up phone calls to schedule appointments from network letters mailed the previous Monday.
2. Conduct information interviews with 2 family friends/alumni scheduled during previous week.
3. Write letters to referrals provided by contacts seen on this day.
4. Attend regularly scheduled (on whatever day) area alumni chapter meeting and make appointments to visit 3 alumni at their offices next week.
5. Prepare for job interview scheduled tomorrow.

Tuesday
1. Conduct job interview and write thank-you letter.
2. Visit OCS or other local career planning and placement offices to identify job leads and apply for any that are appropriate.
3. Conduct information interviews with 2 contacts scheduled during previous week.
4. Write letters to referrals provided by contacts seen on this day.
5. Place follow-up phone calls to schedule appointments from network letters mailed the previous Tuesday.
6. Write thank-you letters for information interviews held on Monday and Tuesday.

Wednesday
1. Take the day off and play!!!
2. Tell everyone you talk to what type of position you are seeking and ask them for advice.

(next page for rest of week)

ORGANIZING YOUR JOB SEARCH (CONTINUED)

Thursday

1. Conduct information interviews with 2 contacts scheduled during the previous week.
2. Write letters to referrals provided by contacts seen on this day.
3. Place follow-up phone calls to schedule appointments from network letters mailed the previous Thursday.
4. Read bimonthly professional journal or area business magazine and list organizations and professionals of interest. Write and mail letters of introduction to targets.
5. Prepare for job interview scheduled tomorrow.

Friday

1. Conduct information interviews with 2 contacts scheduled during the previous week.
2. Write letters to referrals provided by contacts seen on this day.
3. Place follow-up phone calls to schedule appointments from network letters mailed the previous Friday.
4. Follow up with phone calls any advertisements from Sunday's newspaper to which you applied and try to schedule an interview.
5. Conduct job interview and write thank-you letters.
6. Write thank-you notes for information sessions held on Thursday and Friday.

Saturday

1. Take your interviewing outfits to the cleaners.
2. Take the day off: do something that has nothing to do with your job search.

QUANTIFYING YOUR JOB SEARCH

Adhering to a calendar such as this will yield the following weekly results:
*You will have applied for at least 5 job opportunities from newspaper ads, the OCS job listing, and your personal contact network.
*You will have initiated contact with up to 15 new networking prospects.
*You will have conducted at least 8 information sessions.
*You will have completed at least 2 job interviews.
*You will have placed at least 20 job-related phone calls.
*You will have written at least 10 thank-you letters.

Adapted from University of Virginia Office of Career Planning and Placement job-search material developed by Nevin Kessler and Andrew Ceperley.

Chapter 6

❧

Considerations for International Students

If you are an international student without a "green card," you will probably face additional obstacles in getting U.S. nonacademic employment. This chapter addresses some of the issues and hurdles you may encounter. It is not meant to unduly discourage you, but rather to give you ways to maximize your strengths, adapt to American cultural expectations, and overcome possible additional stereotypes about "foreigners." You might also want to read other sources on working in the U.S., such as *Living in the USA* by Alison Lanier.

Visa Regulations

First, a word about Immigration and Nationalization Service (INS) work-related visa requirements. As you undoubtedly know, your student visa (either F-1 or J-1) restricts your post-degree employment to "practical training" in jobs closely related to your field of study, usually for 12 months following your "completion of studies." Options for work *during* your studies are at present both more and less restrictive than postgraduate work: you have wider latitude with the type of work but very limited access to off-campus jobs. Because the regulations change and details are so critical, no specifics are given here, but it is strongly recommended that you meet with one of the advisers at the Harvard International Office (HIO) so that you are absolutely clear about your constraints and the procedures you and your potential employer must follow. By communicating clear and easy guidelines to a potential employer, you will enhance your job prospects.

If you are seeking longer-term employment, you will probably need an H-1B visa, designated for individuals temporarily performing services in a specialty occupation, i.e., one "which requires theoretical and practical application of a body of highly specialized knowledge." The employer must provide documentary evidence that the job requires a person with special qualifications and that the foreign scholar has those qualifications. Recent changes in the law make the process more cumbersome by involving the Department of Labor. Many large, high-tech, and international companies have procedures in place for hiring foreign nationals, but you may still need to convince a potential employer that it's worth the effort.

Canadian citizens can apply for a TC-1 visa if they have a "professional level" job. Certain citizens of the People's Republic of China (PRC) are allowed to work in the U.S. under former President Bush's Executive Order until January 1, 1994, but must also apply through the INS for an employment authorization document (EAD). Moreover, many of these students may be eligible to apply for permanent residence after July 1, 1993 under the Chinese Student Protection Act. (Contact the HIO for more information.)

Naturally, if you are a U.S. citizen or have a green card, you flaunt it; you indicate it on your resume and probably also in your cover letter.

Maximizing Job Opportunities

Because of the visa regulations and other potential hurdles, you maximize your chances by seeking jobs related to your training in areas where labor is in short supply—currently in health sciences, high-tech industries (e.g., computers, biotech), and some engineering and environmental fields. Also look for companies where you have a comparative advantage, for example, multinational corporations doing business in your home country or region, or large companies with multiethnic workforces. Many quasi-academic jobs also require the regional or other substantive expertise that you possess. Look also for organizations with experience in hiring foreign nationals, or for fast-growing, flexible start-up companies. Finally, don't hesitate to find and utilize contacts—individuals and organizations—from your country or ethnic group now in the U.S.

Common Cultural Barriers to the Job Search

Obviously, American cultural attitudes and behaviors related to job hunting and working may be more or less alien to those of your own culture. If you have not thoroughly absorbed American work-related cultural values and expectations, you may want to read this section, which addresses some possible cultural barriers to an effective job search.

1. *Self-promotion.* It's undoubtedly clear by now that a job search in the U.S. requires confidence in discussing your goals and accomplishments and assertiveness in making your case, initiating calls, and following up with all contacts and interviewers. Of course, you don't want to cross over the line into aggressive and arrogant behavior, but your cultural norms may push you in the opposite direction of passivity or diffidence. If in doubt, check out your self-presentation and job-search strategy with a career counselor and/or an American acquaintance with successful job-hunting experience.

2. *Directness in communication.* As discussed in Chapter 5, interviewers expect open and direct responses to questions and a firm handshake, eye contact, and a confident but relaxed posture. If these are uncomfortable for you, practice with American friends or develop strategies around them (e.g., looking at the spot between the eyes). Space is another culturally conditioned concept; take your cues from the interviewer about how close to stand or sit to him or her, but check this out with American friends beforehand.

3. *Self-disclosure.* Many cultures consider personal questions about likes and dislikes or strengths and weaknesses as an invasion of privacy by all except family and close friends. As you know, you will probably be asked to disclose along these lines in an interview. Preparation should enable you to do this more comfortably.

4. *Career self-awareness.* In many countries, personal predilection is a minor factor in choosing a career or in advancing within one. Here you are expected to demonstrate knowledge of yourself, your career goals, and how they relate to the job. If you have taken this book to heart, you should have no problem with this.

5. *Individual responsibility in finding employment.* Although personal and professional networks are very important in finding jobs in the U.S., in general, you must *create* them, rather than—as may be the case in your culture—identify already established family or government or education connections that lead to jobs. So, as you already know, you have to put great effort into generating a wide variety of resources in order to identify *multiple* job possibilities. If it's any consolation, this comes as a surprise to most Americans, too.

6. *Language barriers.* If you do not speak English fairly fluently, you need to practice seriously and regularly, with English-speaking friends, with tapes, in classes, or with a tutor. It is important to practice interviewing; get an American friend to record on tape your answers to imagined questions, and practice the phrasing and inflections, etc. But do not memorize your answers.

It is, of course, much harder to become practiced at interpreting intentions and implications behind verbal utterances and the nonverbal cues of body language. If you are aware of these elements, you can ask American friends to explain ambiguous interactions with interviewers and eventually you will pick up these cues at a less conscious level. Remember, too, that Americans expect you to respond with facial expressions and gestures indicating interest, enthusiasm, and other qualities you want to project. Videotaped mock interviews would be especially instructive, if you are not yet at ease in American work settings.

7. *Two-way stereotypes.* Stereotypes that limit the "objectivity" of both interviewers and interviewees are almost inevitable. You can best deal with this issue by examining your own stereotypes of Americans, as well as of the particular work culture you are interviewing for, and by imagining what the stereotypes of the potential employer toward you might be. Then, as discussed in Chapter 4 in relation to business/academic stereotypes, try in the interview to indirectly counter the biases and fears that seem to underlie certain questions or actions, or in some cases confront them directly in your cover letter or the interview. For example,

if you're from a culture where work rhythms are more relaxed, you may want to mention your acculturation to the American pace of life and work, as exemplified by relevant work or non-work experiences. You will need to have a convincing argument for wanting to remain in the U.S. for career reasons. Even more difficult, if you are seeking practical training only, you will have to counter the employer's bias against hiring and training for just a year. There is no obvious response beyond assuring them that you learn quickly and would like to stay longer and that the INS process is manageable. Finally, it is always a good strategy to stress both your unique strengths and qualities as an individual and the special contribution you can make *because of* your international background.

Common Practical Obstacles

1. *Lack of work experience, especially in the U.S.* Because of visa restrictions and the demands of your studies, you may have little or no work experience in the U.S. Thus, you are especially well advised to find or create internships, freelance opportunities, and/or summer practical training jobs (refer to Chapter 4). If you have no experience in the U.S., you can demonstrate the applicability of your work experience at home or your extracurricular experience in the States.

2. *Lack of a Social Security card.* You must have one in order to work. In order to obtain one, bring your visa and work authorization document to the nearest U.S. Government Social Security Office. The Harvard International Office can help you with this process.

3. *Lack of a car.* This may seem obvious, but do not turn down an interview opportunity for lack of transportation. Check out public transportation or borrow or rent a car if necessary. If you get the job, inquire at human resources for car-pool information. You might even consider buying an inexpensive used car. (Note, however, that employers cannot legally refuse to hire you because you don't have a car, unless the job description explicitly requires one.)

4. *Lack of appropriate interview dress.* It is essential to invest in at least one versatile, professional-looking interview outfit (including shoes). Make sure everything is clean, neat, pressed, polished, etc.

5. *Inappropriate resume and cover letter.* Expectations for resumes vary by country; for example, personal information such as your date of birth or marital status is a must on European resumes, whereas it is discouraged in the U.S. You need, therefore, to be doubly diligent in composing your resume and cover letters. Ask for advice from a career counselor, experienced American friends, and career advisers.

In general it is very important to *start early, pursue multiple options, be flexible, and maintain a positive but realistic attitude.* You may not feel completely yourself in a foreign culture, but strive to convey a sense of your self-worth, as well as your ability to add special value to the company or organization in question.

Vineer Bhansali, an Indian citizen who received his Ph.D. in Theoretical Physics in 1992, ended up with two job offers from investment banking firms (his resume is on pp. 72-73). The offers came after a good deal of soul-searching but only a couple of months of active job hunting. He acknowledges the special obstacles for foreign students, even for someone like himself, who is a native English speaker and has a stellar scientific background: the INS rules discourage the employer from hiring and make job mobility difficult once you are hired. But he found that investment banking offered a "meritocratic" environment, where he didn't have to re-package himself as an American. He concludes:

> In general, the moral from my short experience is that having a different, diverse background is an asset and not a handicap. Present it as such and assert that the very fact that you were able to carry out your program of research in a novel cultural environment points to your adaptability and self-confidence: most honest employers seem to like it. Ask for what you think you deserve for your skills, and don't apologize for not being American; in my experience, if you are looking at a place where your skills will be recognized and put to use, this will never even come up.[1]

1. Vineer Bhansali, letter to the author, January 6, 1993.

Chapter 7

❧

Job Negotiation and Making the Transition

Is that the sound of corks popping? You deserve to celebrate, having landed the job you wanted. But it's not quite time to rest on your laurels. This chapter takes you through the process of negotiating your job offer and offers some advice on easing into your new job.

Job Negotiation

If this *is* essentially the job you want, evaluate whether the offer itself is completely satisfactory. Do you need to negotiate some aspects of it, such as starting date, salary, bonuses, benefits, job responsibilities, and "perks" (e.g., office space, computer equipment, moving expenses, parking)? Whether and how hard you negotiate will depend on several factors, including: (1) your temperament, (2) the norms of the company and industry, (3) the importance to you of the issues at stake, (4) your alternatives, and (5) your assessment of *their* alternatives and interests.

Preparation. As in all previous phases, preparation is time well spent.[1]

---

1. You may want to consult *Getting To Yes* by Roger Fisher and William Ury, many of whose principles are incorporated here.

1. *Think about your interests.* How much do you want the job? How important are various negotiable aspects of the job? How risk-averse are you? By negotiating too aggressively, you may be risking your future relations with your boss and colleagues or conceivably inviting a retraction of the offer; negotiating too timidly may cost you valuable job elements and can even leave a negative impression in some environments.

2. *Think about* **their** *interests.* Try to anticipate their perceptions, values, interests, and constraints. What are their alternatives? How much discretion do they have in fashioning job offers at your level? You'll be fortunate if you have a source of inside information about the search process and competition. Otherwise, assume they have strong alternative candidates.

3. *View the prospective negotiations as a search for mutual gain rather than an automatic "you win/I lose" (zero-sum) situation.* Your future boss is not an adversary, but a potential ally and colleague, with whom you are likely to have many more shared goals and interests than conflicting ones.

4. *Use objective criteria to justify your requests.* The use of objective standards or principles (such as comparability, fairness, obvious need) greatly reduces the effects of personality, arbitrary will, and relative power in the negotiation.

5. *Find out the likely salary range, advancement schedules, and benefits for this and/or similar positions in the particular geographical area.* Sources of information include your network, some human resources offices, professional associations (which will often list minimum standards by state), trade publications, and published job listings.

6. *Know your BATNA* (Best Alternative to a Negotiated Agreement). The possibilities are:

a. You have *no good alternatives*—either no other offers or clearly inferior ones. If you are risk-averse or completely satisfied, you may not want to negotiate at all; otherwise, given that they want you to join them, there is no reason not to try. *They* do not need to know you have no other good options, though you should not lie if asked directly. In any case, you intend to accept their initial offer if necessary.

b. You have *one or more credible alternatives.* Your choice will depend at least partly on the exact offer or package negotiated. This is an enviable position, but you need to be clear about your priorities. What

conditions must be met to make this job the most attractive one?
c. You have a *superior alternative.* Although you could negotiate
over the less preferred offer for the sole purpose of extracting a better offer
from the preferred institution or company, this strategy is ethically
questionable and very risky, especially in a small industry where word
gets around.

7. *Consider your own strengths.* This is clearly related to calculating your BATNA, but even if you have no credible alternatives, knowing
and emphasizing your strengths can be helpful, particularly when they
dovetail with the particular needs of the employer making the offer. Bear
in mind that you will be in your strongest position during the period
between receiving and accepting the offer.

8. *Find your own style.* You may find it difficult to strike a balance
between an overly passive negotiating posture, which is common among
graduate students, and a too aggressive one. (The definition of those terms
will, of course, vary by field/industry and organization.) In general, use
negotiation as a problem-solving method rather than as a game or
adversarial process, and adopt whatever style feels right and natural to
you.

The negotiation process. When negotiating, it is wise to be
straightforward, matter-of-fact, and honest; you don't have to reveal your
BATNA or bottom line (though there may be circumstances where you
want to), but you should never deceive in a way that would damage your
credibility in the future. Don't be too "hard" (aggressive, nasty), but do
convey a healthy sense of self-worth and respect. *Explain and justify your
interests* as you make your request(s). *Listen carefully* to your potential
employer to get additional information on their interests and constraints;
do not press on matters beyond their control. You can use any leverage
you actually have (e.g., "I really want to come here, but —— has offered
me x, y, and z. Is there anything you can do to make it easier to turn them
down?"). How far you go beyond that will depend on you, but bear in mind
that bluffing always carries risks. Finally, silence can be an effective tool,
especially in face-to-face negotiations or if you are presented with an
unsatisfactory offer (e.g., the salary is too low). Simply sit silently for a
few moments, waiting for the employer to jump in with a better offer.

In some environments where traditional "hard" bargaining is the
norm, it may make sense to ask for more than you expect to get so you will

have items on which to "compromise." In general, however, the "softer" approach outlined here is considered most effective.

In the spirit of a joint venture for mutual gain, *look for common interests* behind seemingly conflicting positions. Work with your potential boss to *generate creative options and solutions* to your different positions or even interests. For example, the employer is sympathetic to your need for a couple of months' lead-time to wrap up your current commitments, but needs someone to start almost immediately in order to attend a critical conference. How about your starting part time through the conference and then taking a break before starting full time? Or working part time for the first few months? Or suppose you think your degree is worth more salary than they are prepared to pay (for whatever reason). Might they be willing to increase certain benefits as a tradeoff? Or agree (in writing) to give you a salary review in six months assuming good performance (with the criteria specified in advance)?

Negotiations will most likely be conducted in stages, and you may introduce new requests or change priorities during the process. But don't do this lightly, as this kind of pattern might frustrate the employer. It may be effective to relegate a sticky issue to the back burner while you brainstorm other possibilities and build momentum by getting agreement on the easy issues. Throughout the process, maintain and convey to the employer an enthusiasm for the job, the organization, and your potential employment there.

Once the negotiations are complete, reiterate the offer as you now understand it. Confirm that they will send the offer in writing and indicate your intention to accept as soon as you receive the letter or contract. Also express your appreciation of the employer's willingness to respond to your concerns. If you are not going to accept, explain why as tactfully, honestly, and constructively as possible. Reiterate your positive impressions and your regret that the job didn't work out, and write a follow-up letter as well. In short, whether you accept the job or not, leave them with a positive impression of you.

If you are waiting for other offers, ask whether you can have a little extra time to make the final decision, using your judgment about how much of the situation to explain (but do not lie). If you are pressed for a decision before other offers are made, call the other potential employer(s), explain your situation, and ask whether they can expedite their decision making. Try also to get an accurate assessment of your chances there, to maximize your information in the event that you must decide on one offer before receiving any others. In this difficult situation, gather as much information as possible, try to generate new alternatives, clarify your goals and values with someone you trust, and listen to your intuition as well as your reason. Only *you* can decide, however. If possible, sleep on your decision and see how it feels the next morning.

The follow-up. Professional ethics dictate that once you have accepted a job offer, you are bound to that decision. Although rare exceptions occur, you should make the decision as though it were your final one. Once the decision is formalized, inform all other potential employers that you are no longer on the market, at least for the time being. This is the time to write your entire network to inform them of your good fortune and thank them again for their help. And now, hopefully, you can take that well-deserved vacation before you start the new job!

Making the Transition

Any transition to a new job is stressful, no matter how perfect the job and the "honeymoon" period, and entering a new field is likely to increase the challenge and the level of stress. Here are a few tips to help ease your transition.[2]

1. *Watch, listen, ask, learn before you jump in.* Take some time to absorb and "learn" the formal structure of the organization and, more importantly, the informal organization (e.g., communication and power networks, coalitions) and its culture. Notice how it differs from the academic culture. Observe and try to understand the operating stereotypes, politics, possible glass walls and ceilings, and norms of behavior, dress, and speech *before* you decide how you will react to them. You may want to keep a (very private) journal of your observations.

2. *Get to know your peers, subordinates, and superiors.* Maintain visibility. Establish a strong bond with your secretary and other support

2. Many of these tips were adapted from the following: Deborah Flores, "When You're the New Kid on the Block," *Woman Engineer* (Fall 1991); Christine Kowalke, "Challenges Facing Women in the Workforce," *Careers and the College Grad* (1992); and George Odiorne, "Seven Keys to Managing a Successful Entry Into a New Position," *George Odiorne Letter* (MBO, Inc.) (June 21, 1991).

staff. Schedule regular meetings with your supervisor and begin enlisting him or her as an ally. Do the same with your staff, if you have one, and colleagues.

3. *Focus mainly on your own job* (as opposed to other people's jobs or where you'd like to go). Be clear about your job objectives. Read your predecessor's files, master the routine aspects of the job, identify and prioritize your needs, analyze the problems, and set out to solve them. After you have earned the trust of your co-workers and staff, you can begin to think about innovation and your career advancement in the organization.

4. *Work hard but fruitfully.* Set realistic goals and meet deadlines. It's better to over-deliver than to under-deliver on your commitments. Learn from your inevitable mistakes.

5. *Remain positive and enthusiastic*, generous with praise, and reticent with criticism, complaints, and gossip.

6. *Create a comfortable, practical, and aesthetically pleasing work environment.* Don't underestimate the impact of the aesthetic element on your energy and state of mind nor your ability to transform even a dreary, dinky space with photographs, posters, artwork and art objects, plants, and flowers.

7. *Bear in mind that starting a new job is EXHAUSTING.* Processing all the new external stimuli as well as your internal, possibly unacknowledged "performance anxiety" takes its toll. *Be good to yourself and keep your work in balance with the rest of your life.* Don't give up your sleep, exercise, relationships, or outside interests, and even consider some new ways to keep yourself healthy, happy, and wise.

8. *Remember that you've simply taken the next step and that few life choices are perfect, irrevocable, or final.* What you seek in a job will change over time, so stay in tune with your work values, motivations, and goals. As Bob Bondaryk, a Ph.D. in Biological Chemistry who recently founded his own company, LifeTech Capital, Inc., points out: "It comes down to understanding why you're doing what you're doing (is it interesting? satisfying? remunerative?) and realizing that, at any moment, if you don't like what you're doing, you can get off the train and do something else." [3]

---

3. From a panel on Alternatives to Bench Careers for Scientists, held at OCS, March 3, 1992.

9. *Remember, finally, that any job offers you a chance to build your skills, to make contacts, to learn about an organization, and to establish a record of accomplishment*—all of which will contribute to your success and fulfillment in a career outside the ivory tower.

Bibliography

This bibliography contains a selective listing of books and directories only, though it points you to directories for periodicals and other resources. Most of the entries were taken, with annotations, from Susan Vacca's bibliography in *The Harvard Guide to Careers*. Annotations are supplied only for books reviewed by either Margaret Newhouse or Susan Vacca. Virtually all of these books are currently in print.

I. SELF-ASSESSMENT/CAREER PLANNING

Bridges to Success: Finding Jobs and Changing Careers. Margaret Faughan Austin and Harriet Mason Vines. John Wiley & Sons, Inc., New York, NY, 1983.
  Though rather outdated, contains a good section on self-assessment, in addition to practical job-search information. Extensive bibliography.

Career Planning Today, 2nd edition. C.R. Powell. Kendall-Hunt, Dubuque, IA, 1990.
  Basic, unusually detailed, fairly reliable though business-oriented guide. The cartoons may be difficult to swallow.

Do What You Love, The Money Will Follow. Marsga Sinetar. Dell, New York, NY, 1989.
  This best seller focuses on psychological preparation and self-assessment.

In Transition. Mary Lindley Burton and Richard A. Wedermeyer. Harper Business, New York, NY, 1991.
  This book grew out of a workshop series sponsored by the New York City Harvard Business School Alumni Association for career- and job-changing managers and executives. Despite its business perspective, this is a valuable all-purpose self-assessment, job exploration, and job-search manual, especially for older career changers.

Kissing the Dragon: The Intelligent Work-Hunter's Companion. Madeleine Pelner Cosman. Bard Hall Press, Tenafly, NJ, 1984.
  Somewhat offbeat guide, aimed at self-assessment for Ph.D.'s who are exploring nonacademic careers. There's probably an idea or two in it for anyone. Particularly useful for Humanities Ph.D.'s. Must be ordered directly from the publisher.

The Lotus and the Pool. Hilda Lee Dail. Shambhala Press, Boston, MA, 1989.
Holistic approach with some interesting exercises.

National Directory of Career Resource Centers. Catalyst, New York, NY, no
date.
This pamphlet geographically lists centers that provide career development services and programs, including three international listings. Includes a Catalyst publications list. Updated by a two-sheet supplement in
March 1990. Useful also as a source of job possibilities in career
counseling and development.

*Playing Hardball with Soft Skills: How to Prosper with Non-Technical Skills
in a High-Tech World.* Steven J. Bennett. Bantam Books, New York, NY, 1986.
Although aimed primarily at the individual contemplating an entrepreneurial venture, the self-assessment suggestions can benefit anyone. Good
bibliography.

Self-Assessment and Career Development, 3rd edition. James G. Clawson et al.
Prentice-Hall, Inc., Englewood Cliffs, NJ, 1991.
Stresses self-assessment in combination with career, job, and lifestyle
planning. Excellent appendix of sources of information on selected industries and job and career opportunities. Not a book to be rushed through!

Shifting Gears. Carole Hyatt. S&S Trade, Austin, TX, 1990.

*What Color Is Your Parachute? A Practical Manual for Job-Hunters and Career
Changers.* Richard Nelson Bolles. Ten Speed Press, Berkeley, CA, annual.
Emphasis on exercises as a means of self-evaluation, with listings of
additional sources of information on careers and job hunting. Indexed.

When 9 to 5 Isn't Enough. Marcia Perkins-Reed. Hay House, Inc., Santa
Monica, CA, 1990.
New Age approach combined with practical exercises and advice.

Wishcraft: How to Get What You Really Want. Barbara Sher with Emily
Gottlieb. Ballantine Books, New York, NY, 1986.
A lively and practical self-help manual on setting goals to reach your
dreams.

II. JOB-SEARCH SKILLS AND RESOURCES

The Best Companies for Women. Baila Zeitz and Lorraine Dusky. Simon and Schuster, New York, NY, 1988.

Profiles 50 companies with regard to their policies toward women, including excerpts from interviews with men and women in the companies. Draws some general conclusions in summary chapters. Appendixes list 50 additional companies worth investigating and index the profiled companies geographically (including branches). Name index. Somewhat dated but still useful.

The Complete Job Search Handbook. Howard Figler. Owl Books, Henry Holt & Co., New York, NY, 1988.

This career planning guide is highly recommended at any point in career exploration and job search. The author does an excellent job of simplifying the process. There is advice on assessing skills and interests, job strategies, and interviewing.

CPC National Directory: Who's Who in Career Planning, Placement, and Recruitment. College Placement Council, Inc., Bethlehem, PA, annual.

Lists recruiting personnel at colleges and corporate and government college relations/human resources recruitment personnel. Geographic index of employers.

Educational Opportunities of Greater Boston for Adults: A Comprehensive Directory of Day and Evening Classes. The Education Resources Institute, Boston, MA, annual.

Lists adult and continuing education courses throughout the metropolitan Boston area. Includes schedules and costs. Use not only for sources of additional training but also for ideas for unconventional teaching or administrative positions.

Essentials of Accounting, 4th edition. Robert N. Anthony. Addison-Wesley Publishing Co., Reading, MA, 1988.

A programmed text requiring about 25 hours to complete, including tests. Covers the basic concepts of accounting.

Finding a Job in Your Field: A Handbook for Ph.D.'s and M.A.'s. Rebecca Anthony and Gerald Roe. Peterson's Guides, Princeton, NJ, 1984.

Academic and nonacademic job-search strategies for graduate degree holders. Includes chapters dealing specifically with c.v.'s and resumes and interviewing strategies. Older resource (no longer in print) but information and examples remain useful, if available in a library.

Getting To Yes. Roger Fisher and William Ury. Penguin Books, New York, NY, 1981.

Harcourt Brace Jovanovich College Outline Series. Harcourt Brace Jovanovich, New York, NY.
> Volumes on computers, statistics, etc., offer course material in outline form, along with sample problems and tests.

Internships: On-the-Job Training Opportunities for Students and Adults. Peterson's Guides, Princeton, NJ, annual.
> Includes international listings and introductory information on internships. Lists internship referral and placement services. Geographic and employer indexes.

The *JobBank* series (various cities and regions in the U.S.). Bob Adams, Inc., Holbrook, MA.

Kiplinger's Take Charge of Your Career. Daniel Moreau. Kiplinger Books, Washington, DC, 1990.
> Discusses self-assessment and the job search for the mid-career searcher, with chapters on interviewing, evaluating offers, and fitting in with a new corporate culture. A separate chapter lists the best jobs and places. Indexed.

Knock 'Em Dead with Great Answers to Tough Interview Questions. Martin John Yate. Bob Adams, Inc., Holbrook, MA, 1992.
> Strategies on how to get, survive, and follow up on the interview. Contains a bibliography and an index to the questions.

Living in the USA. Alison Lanier. Intercultural Press, Yarmouth, ME, 1988.

The National Directory of Internships. Barbara E. Baker and Bridget B. Millsaps, editors. National Society for Internships and Experiential Education, Raleigh, NC, 1991.
> Internships and fellowships arranged by type of organization. Alphabetical, geographic, and field indexes.

Places Rated Almanac: Your Guide to Finding the Best Places to Live in America. Richard Boyer and David Savageau. Prentice Hall, New York, NY, 1989.
> Describes and ranks U.S. metropolitan areas on various factors. A good place to begin when contemplating a change of scenery.

Resumes That Work. Tom Cowan. New American Library, New York, NY, 1993.
Sample resumes for different types of job seekers and career fields. Sample
cover letters.

Robert Half on Hiring. Robert Half. Plume [Crown Publishers, Inc.], New
York, NY, 1985.

Schaum's Outline Series. McGraw-Hill Book Co., New York, NY. Various,
many still in print.
Numerous titles in the fields of accounting, business and economics,
computers, mathematics, statistics, etc. Each outline gives basic theory,
definitions, and sample problems.

Sweaty Palms: The Neglected Art of Being Interviewed. H. Anthony Medley.
Ten Speed Press, Berkeley, CA, 1992.
A guide to the entire job-interview process from preparation to follow-up.
Such topics as how to dress and salary discussions. Helpful appendixes on
commonly asked questions, evaluation factors used by interviewers, and
questions asked by interviewers when they check your references. Bibliography.

III. CAREER LITERATURE AND RESOURCES:
General and by Field

1. *General Handbooks, Directories, Indexes, and Career Descriptive Literature*

The American Almanac of Jobs and Salaries. John W. Wright. Avon, New York,
NY, 1990.
Examines various positions in the public, private, and nonprofit sectors,
with salary information taken from Department of Labor and Department
of Commerce data.

Books in Print. R.R. Bowker Co., New York, NY, annual. Updated by Books
in Print Supplement.
Books in Print, the basic source of information concerning books offered
for sale by distributors and publishers in the United States, includes author
and title listings. There is a separate, subject-classified *Subject Guide to
Books in Print*, where career-relevant publications are listed under Library
of Congress subject headings. This resource can be found in most book-
stores, as well as in library reference collections.

Career Advisor Series. Gale Research Inc., Detroit, MI.
　Covers fifteen different career fields. Each guide is packed with information about the field and ideas for getting started, including lists of potential employers, internships, and sources of further information.

A Career Guide for PhD's and PhD Candidates in English and Foreign Languages. Revised by English Showalter. Modern Language Association of America, New York, NY, 1985.
　Describes both academic and nonacademic job searches, with sample letters, c.v.'s, and resumes. Lists some additional resources.

Careers in Information. Jane F. Spivack. Knowledge Industry Publications, Inc., White Plains, NY, 1982.
　Explores entry into the "information" field from a variety of backgrounds: computer science, library science, information science, management and accounting, engineering, communications, and journalism. A good introduction to a career field particularly hospitable to liberal arts and arts and sciences graduates.

Catalyst Career Opportunity Series. Catalyst, New York, NY, 1987.
　Forty briefs and two career planning booklets with information about different occupations. Each career brief is divided into two sections. The first provides an in-depth and candid look at an occupation by profiling an individual in a specific job; the second gives "fast facts" about the industry in general, including the salary level and the education and training needed to enter the field. The two career planning booklets give an overview of the process of career planning.

Creative Careers: Real Jobs in Glamour Fields. Gary Blake and Robert W. Bly. John Wiley & Sons, Inc., New York, NY, 1985.
　An introduction to advertising, book publishing, finance, gourmet food, movies, music, photography, television, theater, travel, and tourism. Includes resources and glossaries.

Dictionary of Occupational Titles, 4th edition. U.S. Department of Labor, U.S. Employment Service, U.S. Government Printing Office, Washington, DC, 1977.
　Contains almost 17,500 job titles and their definitions, arranged by type of occupation. A good way to get an overview of the different job possibilities within a given field, although not all will be of interest to the liberal arts graduate. Occupational title and industry indexes. DOT Supplement published in 1982; includes many high-tech titles.

Directories in Print. Julie E. Towell & Charles B. Montney, editors. Gale Research, Inc., Detroit, MI, bienniel.
> An invaluable annotated guide to about 10,000 directories published in the U.S. and Canada. Arranged in 16 major subject categories. Includes computer-readable formats. Title/keyword and subject indexes.

Directory of Counseling Services. Nancy E. Roncketti, editor. International Association of Counseling Services, Alexandria, VA, annual.
> Listing of the association's member organizations in the U.S. and Canada, including those at colleges and universities.

Directory of U.S. International Health Organizations. The National Council for International Health, Washington, DC, 1992.
> Alphabetical listing of organizations. Lists contact. Classifies organizations by country and activity.

Encyclopedia of Associations. Gale Research, Inc., Detroit, MI, annual. 3 volumes.
> Volume 1 provides details on active nonprofit organizations of national scope, arranged in 18 subject categories, with name and keyword index. Volume 2 is a geographic and executive index to volume 1. Volume 3 supplements volume 1.

Foreign Languages and Your Career, 3rd edition. Edward Bourgoin. Columbia Languages Services, Washington, DC, 1984.
> Introduces the various career fields in which foreign language skills are important or necessary. Lists additional sources of information, including organizations. Index of occupations.

Funding for Research, Study, and Travel: (various countries). Karen Cantrell and Denise Wallen, editors. Oryx Press, Phoenix, AZ, 1987.
> Alphabetically arranged by sponsor, with subject and sponsor type indexes. Annotated bibliography includes online databases.

The Harvard Guide to Careers. Martha P. Leape and Susan M. Vacca. Office of Career Services, Faculty of Arts and Sciences, Harvard University, distributed by Harvard University Press, Cambridge, MA, 1991.
> General guide to career exploration and job hunting, geared to liberal arts graduates and graduate students in the arts and sciences. Includes sample resumes and letters. Extensive annotated bibliographies.

Humanities Ph.D.'s and Nonacademic Careers. Roger E. Wyman and Nancy A. Riser. The Committee on Institutional Cooperation, Evanston, IL, 1984.

Jobs for English Majors and Other Smart People, 3rd edition. Peterson's Guides, Princeton, NJ, 1991.

Jobs '93. Kathryn and Ross Petras. Prentice Hall Press, New York, NY, annual.
Contains career outlooks by field, industry forecasts, and a regional profile
of employment prospects. Lists additional sources of information, as well
as major employers by industry and state. Special reports on women,
minorities, and disabled workers. (Title changes with year.)

National Trade and Professional Associations of the United States. Columbia
Books, Inc., Washington, DC, annual.
Overlaps with *Encyclopedia of Associations* in some ways, but often
provides different kinds of information. Information about headquarters,
chief officers, activities, and publications is usually given. Keyword and
geographical indexes make it easier to find associations connected with a
given field or based in a certain geographical area.

*The New Careers Directory: A Directory of Jobs and Internships in Technology
and Society*, 4th edition. Rachel Helfand, editor. Student Pugwash USA,
Washington, DC, 1993.
Aimed at helping students and recent graduates—with or without scientific
training—to locate internship and entry-level employment opportunities.
Contains advice for interns, bibliography, and separate sections on jobs and
internships with the government. Geographical and issue area indexes.

The New York Times Index. New York Times Co., New York, NY, semimonthly
with quarterly and annual cumulations.

Occupational Outlook Handbook. U.S. Department of Labor, Bureau of Labor
Statistics, Government Printing Office, Washington, DC, biennial.
Describes in detail about 250 occupations. Keyed numerically to the
Dictionary of Occupational Titles, this book describes the nature of the
work conditions, training, employment outlook, earnings, and related
occupations. Lists sources of additional information.

Occupational Outlook Quarterly. U.S. Department of Labor, Bureau of Labor
Statistics, Occupational Outlook Service, Washington, DC, quarterly.
Contains articles on new occupations, training opportunities, salary trends,
career counseling programs, etc.

The 100 Best Companies to Work for in America. Robert Levering et al.
Addison-Wesley Publishing Co., Reading, MA, 1993.
Alphabetically lists and describes the companies, rating them in terms of
pay, benefits, job security, advancement, and ambience. Gives one major
advantage and one major disadvantage for each company, and ranks
companies on just about any criterion you can think of.

Opportunities in Foreign Language Careers. Edwin Arnold and Theodore Huebener. VGM Career Horizons, Lincolnwood, IL, 1992.

Part-Time Professional. Diane S. Rothberg & Barbara Ensor Cook. Acropolis Books Ltd., Washington, DC, 1985.

> Profiles individuals and a limited number of employers in the private sector. Explores part-time employment with government agencies. Discusses relevant issues and strategies for negotiating with employers.

Subject Collections: A Guide to Special Book Collections and Subject Emphases as Reported by University, College, Public and Special Libraries and Museums in the United States, 7th edition. Lee Ash and William C. Miller. R.R. Bowker, New York, NY, 1993.

> As suggested by its title, contains rich ideas for quasi-academic jobs in unusual settings. More than 18,000 collections in over 11,000 academic, public, and special libraries and museums, indexed and cross-referenced under 37,000 subject headings, with publisher annotations.

VGM Professional Careers Series. VGM Career Books, Lincolnwood, IL. Various.

> Separate volumes examine careers in accounting, business, communications, computing, education, engineering, health care, and science. A good way to gain an overview of the various positions and career paths within each field (e.g., *VGM Careers Encyclopedia,* 1991; *VGM Handbook of Business & Management Careers,* 1989; *VGM Handbook of Scientific & Technical Careers,* 1989).

2. Business (including financial services and consulting, but excluding high-tech business)

Business Periodicals Index. H.W. Wilson Co., Bronx, NY, monthly, with annual cumulations.

> Indexes English-language business periodicals, with a separate listing of citations to book reviews. A good way to look up current information on potential employers, assuming you have access to the periodicals indexed.

Careers in Marketing. David W. Rosenthall and Michael A. Powell. Prentice-Hall, Inc., Englewood Cliffs, NJ, 1984.

> Profiles 26 career categories within the marketing field, including non-profit marketing. Includes alternate job titles, position requirements, comments from individuals in each field, bibliographies. Index of job titles.

Choosing a Career in Business. Stephen A. Stumpf and Celeste Kennon Rodgers. Simon & Schuster, New York, NY, 1984.
Examines the required skills and background for various business careers; describes each field and relevant job functions. Includes a chapter on job-hunting strategy. Bibliography.

Consultants and Consulting Organizations Directory: A Reference Guide to Concerns and Individuals Engaged in Consultation for Business, Industry and Government. Janice McLean, editor. Gale Research Inc., Detroit, MI, annual. 2 volumes.
Volume 1 lists firms by field of consulting activity. Geographic, consulting activities, personal name, and consulting firms indexes are contained in volume 2. Updated by *New Consultants.*

Corporate Cultures: The Rites and Rituals of Corporate Life. Terrence E. Deal and Allan A. Kennedy. Addison-Wesley Publishing Co., Reading, MA, 1982.
The title is self-explanatory: examines the corporate sphere in terms of its cultures, values, myths, symbols, and modes of communication. A good, interestingly written introduction to the corporate world. Bibliography. Index.

The Corporate Finance Sourcebook. National Register Publishing Co., Wilmette, IL, annual.
Classified listing of capital funding and management sources, including venture capital firms, banks, pension managers, and accounting firms. Index of firms.

Corporate Ph.D.: Making the Grade in Business. Carol Groneman and Robert N. Lear. Facts on File, New York, NY, 1985.
Profiles of Ph.D.'s who pursued careers in the private sector, and interviews with employers who have hired Ph.D.'s. Stresses the transferability of skills from the academic to the corporate world. Note that business stereotypes toward Ph.D.'s have softened on the whole since 1985.

The Directory of Executive Recruiters. Kennedy Publications, Fitzwilliam, NH, annual.
Introductory information for candidates and clients, followed by separate sections for retainer firms and contingency firms, each indexed by function and industry. Geographic and key principals indexes.

Encyclopedia of Business Information Sources: A Bibliographic Guide to More Than 24,000 Citations Covering Over 1,000 Subjects of Interest to Business Personnel. James Woy, editor. Gale Research Inc., Detroit, MI, biennial.
Includes print, online, organizational, etc., sources of information. An excellent resource for researching a particular business topic or industry.

Growing a Business. Paul Hawken. S&S Trade, Austin, TX, 1988.

Harvard Business School Career Guide: Management Consulting 1993. Harvard Business School Career Resources Center and the Harvard Business School Management Consulting Club, distributed by the Harvard Business School Press, Boston, MA, biennial.
Intended primarily for M.B.A. students, this publication introduces the consulting field, and includes self-descriptions by a number of top firms. Good brief annotated bibliography. Other volumes on marketing and finance.

The Harvard College Guide to Consulting. Marc P. Cosentino. Office of Career Services, Faculty of Arts and Sciences, Harvard University, Cambridge, MA, 1991.
An introductory chapter on consulting in general, followed by essays on the specialties within the field, each written by a practitioner.

The Harvard College Guide to Investment Banking. Marc Cosentino. Office of Career Services, Faculty of Arts and Sciences, Harvard University, Cambridge, MA, 1990.
Chapters on corporate finance, public finance, sales and trading, entry-level positions, and retail brokerage. Includes four appendixes: dilemmas and decisions, internships, sample resumes, and a reading list. Glossary.

How to Become a Successful Consultant in Your Own Field. Hubert Bermont. Prima Publishing, Rocklin, CA, 1991.

National Directory of Corporate Public Affairs. Arthur C. Close et al., editors. Columbia Books, Inc., Washington, DC, annual.
Alphabetical listing of companies with public affairs programs; gives people, addresses, and publications. Separate listing of individuals engaged in public affairs programs. Industry and geographic indexes.

The National Directory of Corporate Training Programs. Ray Bard and Susan K. Elliott. Doubleday, New York, NY, 1988.
Alphabetically arranged by company, with information on recruitment, placement, training, etc. Training program, industry, and geographic indexes. Bibliography. Useful also for exploring possible corporate training jobs.

Pratt's Guide to Venture Capital Sources. Jane K. Morris, Susan Isenstein, and Ann Knowles, editors. Venture Economics, Inc., Needham, MA, annual.

>Excellent introductory section on the venture capital industry, followed by geographically arranged listings of venture capital companies in the U.S. and Canada. Company, name, and industry preference indexes.

Predicasts F&S Index. Predicasts, Cleveland, OH, weekly with monthly, quarterly, and annual cumulations. Volumes for U.S., Europe, and international.

Rating America's Corporate Conscience: A Provocative Guide to the Companies Behind the Products You Buy Every Day. Steven D. Lyndenberg, Alice Tepper Marlin, and Sean O'Brien Strub. Addison-Wesley Publishing Co., Inc., Reading, MA, 1986.

>This publication of the Council on Economic Priorities provides information on the social responsibility records of major American companies, including policies relating to women, minorities, military contracts, PAC contributions, etc. Lists resources. Summary list of company products and services. Indexed.

Reference Book of Corporate Managements. Dun's Marketing Services, Inc., Parsippany, NJ, annual. 4 volumes.

>Biographical profiles of the principal officers in over 12,000 U.S. companies. Arranged alphabetically by company, with geographic, industry, and personal name indexes.

Standard & Poor's Register of Corporations, Directors and Executives. Standard & Poor's Corp., New York, NY, annual, with triennial supplement. 3 volumes.

>Volume 1 lists U.S. corporations alphabetically, naming principal executives. Volume 2 lists directors and executives alphabetically, giving very brief biographical information where available. Volume 3 contains industrial, geographic, and corporate family indexes.

Standard & Poor's Security Dealers of North America. Standard & Poor's Corp., New York, NY, semiannual.

>Geographically arranged, with index of firms. Geographic listing of foreign offices.

Starting on a Shoestring. Building a Business Without a Bankroll. Arnold Goldstein. John Wiley & Sons, Inc., New York, NY, 1991.

Thomson Bank Directory. Thomson Financial Publishing Inc., Skokie, IL, semiannual. 3 volumes.

Volumes 1 and 2 list banks geographically within the U.S. and include names of officers and financial data. Alphabetical index. Volume 3 contains geographic listings of international banks in foreign exchange/trade (other than those in U.S. locations) and has an alphabetical index.

Wall Street Journal Index. University Microfilms International, Ann Arbor, MI, monthly with annual cumulations.

What They Still Don't Teach You at Harvard Business School. Mark H. McCormack. Bantam Books, New York, NY, 1990.

Practical advice on how to function and thrive in the business world. The sections "How to Find Your First Great Job (or What Every Graduate Wants to Know)," "Working for Nothing," and "What Really Happens to Resumes" are worth the price of the book!

3. *Education and Training (including secondary teaching/administration, college/university administration, educational consulting and policy, corporate training and development)*

Directory of Public School Systems in the U.S. Association for School, College and University Staffing, Inc., Addison, IL, annual.

Lists school districts and employing officials by state.

The Handbook of Private Schools: An Annual Descriptive Survey of Independent Education. Porter Sargent Publishers, Inc., Boston, MA, annual.

Geographically arranged listing of leading private schools, with separate listings for schools abroad, summer camps and programs, etc. Index of schools.

The Learning Field: A Guide to Education Services in Greater Boston. Career Planning and Placement Office, Harvard Graduate School of Education, Cambridge, MA, 1993.

A directory of Boston area organizations that try to influence or serve mainstream educational institutions. Categories include advocacy, educational services, educational resources, arts/cultural institutions, media, technology, human resources, research and evaluation, consulting, government, and international. Available from HGSE.

Myths and Realities of Academic Administration. Patricia R. Plante, with Robert L. Caret. American Council on Education. Macmillan Publishing Company, New York, NY, 1991.

Private Independent Schools. Bunting and Lyon, Inc., Wallingford, CT, annual.
Geographically arranged listing includes American programs in other countries and U.S. territories. Separate section for summer programs, including sports, the arts, etc. Index of schools.

Prospects for Faculty in the Arts and Sciences: A Study of Factors Affecting Demand and Supply 1987 to 2012. William G. Bowen and Julie Ann Sosa. Princeton University Press, Princeton, NJ, 1989.

Requirements for Certification of Teachers, Counselors, Librarians, Administrators for Elementary and Secondary Schools. John Tryneski. The University of Chicago Press, Chicago, IL, annual.
Geographically arranged. The appendix lists addresses of state offices of certification.

The Right Fit: An Educator's Career Handbook and Employment Guide. Judy A. Strother and Darrel R. Marshall. Gorusch Scarisbrick, Scottsdale, AZ, 1990.
This outline of the job search for jobs in education includes higher education administration and international teaching and gives many examples. Chapters on c.v.'s, resumes, cover letters, and interviewing.

Training and Development Organizations Directory, 5th edition. Janice McLean, editor. Gale Research Inc., Detroit, MI, 1991.
Alphabetically profiles firms, institutes, etc. Geographic, personal name, and subject indexes.

Training: The Competitive Edge. Jerome Rosow and Robert Zager. Josey-Bass, Work in America Institute, Scarsdale, NY, 1988.

The World of Learning. Europa Publications Limited, London, England, annual.
Geographic arrangement of educational institutions, libraries, learned societies, and scientific and cultural organizations. Separate section on international organizations. Index of institutions.

4. *Government, Policy, Politics, and Law*

The Almanac of American Politics. Michael Barone and Grant Ujifusa. National Journal, Washington, DC, annual.

Contains basic information on elections, individuals, and events, from the Presidency and Congress through the state level. Detailed data on congressional districts and their representatives, and separate chapters on demographics and campaign finance. Indexed.

Congressional Staff Directory. Ann L. Brownson, editor. Congressional Staff Directory, Ltd., Mount Vernon, VA, semiannual.

Information on key personnel of the legislative branch. Congressional staff biographies. Keyword index and index of individuals.

Congressional Yellow Book. Monitor Publishing Co., Washington, DC, quarterly.

Profiles members of Congress and congressional committees. Includes information on aides and congressional support agencies (such as the Library of Congress).

Federal Career Directory. United States Office of Personnel Management. Superintendent of Documents, U.S. Government Printing Office, Washington, DC, 1990.

Describes federal career and employment opportunities, including internship and student employment programs.

Federal Executive Directory. Carroll Publishing Co., Washington, DC, bimonthly.

Telephone numbers, names, addresses, and titles for individuals in the executive branch and Congress. Keyword index.

Federal Regional Executive Directory. Carroll Publishing Co., Washington, DC, semiannual.

Information on federal regional offices, home state offices of members of Congress, key personnel of federal courts, and contacts for military bases. Name, keyword, and geographic indexes.

Federal Regulatory Directory, 6th edition. Congressional Quarterly, Inc., Washington, DC, 1990.

Profiles regulatory agencies within the federal government, including names of contacts. Name and subject indexes.

Federal Yellow Book. Monitor Publishing Co., Washington, DC, quarterly.

Arranged by department or agency, lists names and telephone numbers of top people in the executive branch of the federal government. Indexed.

Government Research Directory. Gale Publishing, Detroit, MI, annual.

The Harvard College Guide to Careers in Government and Politics. Lynn Bracken Wehnes. Office of Career Services, Faculty of Arts and Sciences, Harvard University, Cambridge, MA, 1992.

> A beginner's manual for those contemplating employment in government and politics, with references to additional sources of information for the job seeker. Has a particular emphasis on working in Washington, Foreign Service careers, and campaign work.

Municipal Executive Directory. Wil Woodrum, editor. Carroll Publishing Co., Washington, DC, semiannual.

> Alphabetically lists key executives of over 2,000 municipalities with populations over 1,000. Alphabetical listing of executives. Includes listings for related national associations, state municipal associations, and members of the National Association of Towns and Townships.

Public Interest Profiles, 1991-1993. Foundation for Public Affairs. Congressional Quarterly, Inc., Washington, DC, 1991.

> Profiles public interest and public policy organizations. Arranged by field of interest; includes think tanks. Good coverage of each group provides budget information, staff size, operating method, publication lists, etc. Group and name indexes.

State Municipal League Directory. National League of Cities, Washington, DC, annual.

> Describes the municipal leagues in existence for the continental states. Includes league publications which sometimes carry job opportunities for member municipalities.

State Yellow Book: A Directory of the Executive, Legislative and Judicial Branches of the 50 State Governments. Monitor Publishing Co., New York, NY, semiannual.

> Includes state profiles and intergovernmental organizations. Subject and name (by state) indexes.

The United States Government Manual. Office of the Federal Register, National Archives and Records Administration, Washington, DC, annual.

> Official handbook of the U.S. government. Describes departments and agencies, lists key personnel, and provides organization charts. Names and subject/agency indexes. Includes information on quasi-official agencies, international organizations in which the U.S. participates, boards, committees, and commissions. The place to start for information on the federal government.

WashingtonInformationDirectory. Congressional Quarterly Inc., Washington, DC, annual.

Classified arrangement of information services in the public and nonprofit sectors in the Washington area, including names of officials and brief mission statement. Name and subject indexes.

Washington '93: A Comprehensive Directory of the Key Institutions and Leaders of the National Capital Area. Columbia Books, Inc., Washington, DC, annual.

Classified arrangement of institutions, law firms, the media, governmental units, and other organizations in Washington. Index of organizations and individuals. (Title changes with year.)

Washington Representatives: Who Does What for Whom in the Nation's Capital. Columbia Books, Inc., Washington, DC, annual.

Alphabetical listing of individuals who work for American trade associations, professional societies, labor unions, corporations, and public interest groups, followed by an alphabetical listing of companies and organizations. Subject and foreign interest indexes.

5. *International Careers*

Alternatives to the Peace Corps: Gaining Third World Experience. Institute for Food and Development Policy, San Francisco, CA, 1990.

Introductory information, followed by listings of international and U.S. voluntary service organizations, study tours, and alternative travel groups. Resource lists. Index of organizations.

Careers in International Affairs. Linda L. Powers, editor. School of Foreign Service, Georgetown University, Washington, DC, 1991.

An introduction to international work in a variety of settings, including business, education, government, nonprofits, research, and international organizations. Identifies and describes potential employers and provides addresses. Bibliography. Index.

Complete Guide to International Jobs & Careers, 2nd edition. Ronald L. Krannich & Caryl R. Krannich. Impact, Manassas Park, VA, 1992.

Development Network Opportunities Catalog. Stanford International Development Organization, Overseas Development Network, San Francisco, CA, 1991.

Guide to internships, research, and employment with development organizations. Alphabetically arranged; includes contacts. Geographic index.

Directory of American Firms Operating in Foreign Countries, 12th edition. World Trade Academy Press. Uniworld Business Publications, New York, NY, 1991. 3 volumes.
> Volume 1 contains alphabetical listings of U.S. firms operating overseas providing, in some cases, names of president/CEO, chief foreign officer, and personnel director. Volumes 2 and 3 index firms by country, and include name and U.S. address of parent firm as well as name and address of subsidiary or affiliate in that country.

Directory of Foreign Firms Operating in the United States, 7th edition. World Trade Academy Press. Uniworld Business Publications, Inc., New York, NY, 1992.
> Firms grouped by country, listing their American affiliates. Foreign firm and American affiliate indexes.

The Directory of Jobs and Careers Abroad. Alex Lipinski, editor. Peterson's Guides, Princeton, NJ, 1989.

East-West Business Directory. Duncan University/Carlton Publishing, Ottawa, Canada, annual.

Encyclopedia of Associations: International Organizations. Gale Research Inc., Detroit, MI, 1990.
> Describes international nonprofit membership organizations (including national organizations based outside of the U.S.), and includes geographic, executive, and name and keyword indexes.

European Consultants' Directory. Gale Research Inc., Detroit, MI, annual.

European Technical Consultancies. Daphne M. Tomlinson, consultant editor. Longman, Harlow, England, 1989.
> Lists consulting firms by country (for Western Europe). Companies and acronyms, services, industries served, and personal name indexes.

Fellowships, Scholarships, and Related Opportunities in International Education. Center for International Education, University of Tennessee, Knoxville, TN, 1986.
> Alphabetically arranged; aimed at U.S. citizens and permanent residents. Area of study index. Use to get ideas for organizations involved in international education.

Financial Aid for Research and Creative Activities Abroad and *Financial Aid for Study and Training Abroad.* Gail Ann Schlachter and R. David Weber. Reference Service Press, San Carlos, CA, biennial.

Lists scholarships, fellowships, loans, grants, awards, and internships for high school/undergraduate students, graduate students, postdocs, and professionals/other individuals. Annotated bibliography. Program, sponsoring organization, geographic, subject, and deadline indexes. Also source of ideas for potential jobs at sponsoring organizations.

Financial Resources for International Study: A Definitive Guide to Organizations Offering Awards for Overseas Study. The Institute of International Education. Peterson's Guides, Princeton, NJ, 1989.

Alphabetically arranged by sponsor, with sponsoring institutions, fields of study, and academic level indexes. Introductory chapter on planning international study.

Guide to Careers in World Affairs. Foreign Policy Association, New York, NY, 1992.

The International Corporate 1000: A Directory of Those Who Manage the World's Leading 1000 Corporations. Monitor Publishing Co., New York, NY, annual.

Company listings by region. Parent company, subsidiary, division and affiliate, geographical, industry, and name indexes. Time zone and world holiday charts.

International Directory of Arts. Art Address Verlag Mueller GmbH & Co., Frankfurt am Main, Federal Republic of Germany, biennial. 2 volumes.

Museums, schools, associations, artists, numismatists, art and antique dealers, galleries, auctioneers, restorers, art publishers, periodicals, and antiquarian and art booksellers, each arranged by country.

International Directory of Corporate Affiliations. National Register Publishing Co., Wilmette, IL, annual.

International Jobs: Where They Are, How to Get Them: A Handbook for Over 500 Career Opportunities Around the World. Eric Kocher. Addison-Wesley Publishing Co., Reading, MA, 1983.

Part 1, "International Career Planning and Job Strategy," covers the process of getting a job. Part 2, "The International Job Market," profiles employers across a range of fields, from the federal government through teaching and international law. Bibliography. Index.

International Research Centers Directory. Darren L. Smith, editor. Gale Research Inc., Detroit, MI, biennial.
> Multinational section, followed by listings by country. Name and keyword, country, and subject indexes.

The International Schools Directory. European Council of International Schools, Inc., Petersfield, England, distributed by Peterson's Guides, Inc., Princeton, NJ, annual.
> Profiles member schools geographically. Separate sections for affiliate and supporting member schools. Geographic index gives statistical information on international schools worldwide, including non-ECIS schools. Separate indexes of schools offering boarding facilities and the international baccalaureate.

The ISS Directory of Overseas Schools. International Schools Services, Princeton, NJ, distributed by Peterson's Guides, Princeton, NJ, annual.
> Geographically arranged profiles of American-style primary and secondary schools. Indexes of schools offering the international baccalaureate and schools with boarding facilities. Lists accrediting associations and regional and international organizations. Indexed.

Jobs in Japan, 4th edition. John Wharton. Global Press, Denver, CO, 1991.
> A combination how-to and where-to survival guide. Listings of private English schools.

Looking for Employment in Foreign Countries., 8th edition. June L. Aulick, editor. World Trade Academy Press Inc., New York, NY, 1990.
> General information on working abroad in a variety of settings, followed by brief country profiles. Chapters on resumes and cover letters and interviewing. Indexed.

Moody's International Manual. Moody's Investor's Service, New York, NY, annual.

The Overseas List: Opportunities for Living and Working in Developing Countries. David M. Beckmann et al. Augsburg Publishing House, Minneapolis, MN, 1985.
> Examines employment in the Third World, from public service opportunities to those in the private sector. Includes a chapter on study and tourism. Lists resources throughout. Activities, geographic, and organization indexes.

Schools Abroad of Interest to Americans. Donna Vierra and Heather Lane, editors. Porter Sargent Publishers, Inc., Boston, MA, 1991.
Geographic listing of elementary and secondary schools. Includes some post-secondary schools, specialized opportunities, and summer sessions. Alphabetical index to schools.

Staffing Europe: An Indispensible Guide to Hiring and Being Hired in the New Europe. Max Messer. Acropolis Books Ltd., Herndon, VA, 1991.

Study Abroad. UNESCO, Paris, France, triennial.
Describes international study programs offered by institutions in 126 countries, with section devoted to financial assistance. International organization, institution, subject of study indexes. In English, French, and Spanish. Use as a source for administrative and teaching jobs in international education.

Ulrich's International Periodicals Directory. R.R. Bowker Co., New York, NY, annual, with quarterly updates. 3 volumes.
A subject listing of over 111,000 periodicals from around the world. A particularly helpful feature is the "Subject Guide to Abstracting and Indexing." This will lead to publications which index the periodicals in a particular field. Index to publications of international organizations and title index.

U.S. East European Trade Directory. Probus Publishing Company, Chicago, IL, 1991.

World Chamber of Commerce Directory. World Chamber of Commerce Directory, Inc., Loveland, CO, annual.
Lists chambers of commerce geographically. Includes state boards of tourism, convention and visitors bureaus, and economic development organizations in the U.S., as well as American chambers of commerce abroad, foreign tourist information bureaus, and foreign chambers of commerce in the U.S. A separate section provides listings for the U.S. Congress, dean of diplomatic corps, foreign embassies in the U.S., and U.S. embassies.

Worldwide Government Directory with International Organizations. Cambridge Information Group Directories, Inc., Gaithersburg, MD, annual.
Part 1 is arranged by country and outlines the governmental structure, including the legislative and the judicial, as well as the central bank, UN mission, and major foreign embassies located in the country. Part 2 lists international organizations alphabetically, including United Nations organizations, agencies, commissions, etc.

6. *Media (including creative writing, journalism, editing, publishing, advertising and public relations, corporate communications, film and TV)*

The AWP Official Guide to Writing Programs, 6th edition. D.W. Fenza and Beth Jarock, editors. Associated Writing Programs, Old Dominion University, Norfolk, VA, 1992.

> Profiles writing programs and their faculty in the U.S. and Canada. Also describes writers' centers, colonies, and conferences, including one in Ireland. Geographic and degree indexes.

Career Opportunities for Writers. Rosemary Guiley. Facts on File Publications, New York, NY, 1985.

> Describes 91 jobs in eight major fields, with salary and career development information. Appendixes list: educational institutions; professional, industry, and trade associations and unions; major trade periodicals; bibliography. Job title index.

Career Opportunities in Television, Cable, and Video. Maxine K. Reed and Robert M. Reed. Facts on File Publications, New York, NY, 1986.

> Describes 100 jobs in the field, with salary and career development information. Excellent bibliography.

Careers for Bookworms and Other Literary Types. Marjorie Ebert and Margaret Gisler. VGM Career Horizons, Lincolnwood, IL, 1990.

Editor and Publisher International Yearbook. Editor & Publisher, New York, NY, annual.

> Geographic listings of: daily, weekly, and specialized newspapers in the U.S. and Canada; general interest newspapers in the rest of the world. Includes information on services, organizations, education, foreign correspondents in the U.S., etc. Indexed.

Gale Directory of Publications and Broadcast Media. Gale Research, Inc., Detroit, MI, annual.

> Geographically lists media, including trade journals, radio and television stations, and cable systems in the U.S., Puerto Rico, and Canada, with cross-reference indexes for specific types of publications and radio station format. Includes names, addresses, and telephone numbers of newspaper feature editors. Master name and keyword index.

The Harvard Guide to Careers in Mass Media. John H. Noble. Office of Career Services, Harvard University, Cambridge, MA, distributed by Bob Adams, Inc., Holbrook, MA, 1989.
> Profiles eight career fields within the entertainment media, news media, publishing, and promotional media. Includes annotated bibliographic references, case studies, and job-hunting tips.

Hudson's Subscription Newsletter Directory. Margaret Leonard, editor. Hudson's Newsletter Directory, Rhinebeck, NY, annual.
> Selective listings of subscription newsletters in the U.S. and abroad, by subject and geographic location. A separate section contains information of interest to someone in or considering entering the newsletter trade. Title index.

The International Directory of Little Magazines and Small Presses, 28th edition. Len Fulton, editor. Dustbooks, Paradise, CA, 1992.
> Alphabetical listing, with regional and subject indexes.

Jobs in Arts and Media Management. Stephen Langley and James Abruzzo. ACA Books, New York, NY, 1992.
> Describes the various career fields and offers job-hunting advice. Lists graduate programs in arts administration, arts and media management internships, seminars, workshops, information centers, referral services, membership associations, and periodicals with job listings.

Literary Market Place. R.R. Bowker Co., New York, NY, annual.
> Lists publishers, organizations, events, awards, fellowships and grants, services, etc., for the publishing trade in the U.S. and Canada; includes foreign publishers with U.S. offices. U.S. publishers can be accessed by geographic location, type, and subject matter. Directory of organizations and individuals included in the text (with phone numbers and addresses).

News Media Yellow Book of Washington and New York: A Directory of Those Who Report, Write, Edit and Produce the News in the Nation's Government and Business Capitals. Monitor Publishing Co., New York, NY, semiannual.
> Divided into ten sections: news services, newspapers, networks, stations, programs, periodicals, newsletters, publishers, associations, and foreign media. Assignment (by news beat), syndicated columnist, program (by subject), periodical (by subject), personnel, and media indexes.

O'Dwyer's Directory of Corporate Communications. J.R. O'Dwyer Co., Inc., New York, NY, annual.

> Lists public relations/communications departments of 5,400 companies and associations, including federal government departments, bureaus, agencies, and commissions. Industry and geographic indexes to corporations; geographical index to associations. Includes foreign listings (mostly Canadian).

O'Dwyer's Directory of Public Relations Firms. J.R. O'Dwyer Co., Inc., New York, NY, annual.

> Alphabetical listing of firms; entries include principal executives and clients. Specialty, geographic, and client indexes. Includes firms and branches located outside the U.S.

Standard Directory of Advertisers: The Advertiser Red Book. National Register Publishing Co., Wilmette, IL, 1991. 2 editions annually: classified and geographic.

> Lists companies engaged in national or regional advertising, with product and executive information. Describes advertising agencies and media used, amounts spent, etc. Classified edition has alphabetical and separately published geographic indexes. Updated by *Ad Change*.

Standard Directory of Advertising Agencies: The Agency Red Book. National Register Publishing Co., Wilmette, IL, three times yearly.

> Alphabetical listing of approximately 6,500 agencies, giving size, dollar amount of billings, names of executives, and in many cases identifying accounts. Special market, geographic, and name indexes. Includes foreign agencies and separate listings for house agencies, media service organizations, sales promotion agencies, and public relations firms. Updated by *Agency News*.

Standard Periodical Directory. Oxbridge Communications, Inc., New York, NY, annual.

> A comprehensive directory of U.S. and Canadian periodicals, including trade journals, newsletters, house organs, yearbooks, etc. "Periodical," in this case, refers to any publication issued at least once every two years. Although some of the descriptions are quite sketchy, this is a good place to get some basic information on obscure publications. Title and subject indexes.

7. *Nonprofit (including the arts, public service, social welfare, foundations, and most research organizations, but excluding education and health)*

America's Non Profit Sector: A Primer. Lester M. Salamon. The Foundation Center, New York, NY, 1992.

Artist's Market: Where & How to Sell Your Artwork. Laurie Miller, editor. Writer's Digest Books, Cincinnati, OH, annual.

Introductory chapter on "The Business of Art," followed by a classified listing of the markets, from advertising to syndicates. Includes interviews with successful artists and art buyers. Bibliography, glossary, art/design studio subject and geographic indexes, magazine subject index, general index.

Career Opportunities in Art. Susan H. Haubenstock and David Joselit. Facts on File Publications, New York, NY, 1988.

Describes 75 different positions in the field, with salary and career development information. Appendixes list schools, funding opportunities, professional organizations, and resources. Job title index.

Career Opportunities in the Music Industry. Shelly Field. Facts on File Publications, New York, NY, 1986.

Provides salary, skill requirements, career path, and other information for 79 jobs in the performing, business, and educational areas of the music field. Appendixes list educational programs, organizations, etc., including a glossary. Indexed.

Careers for Culture Lovers & Other Artsy Types. Marjorie Ebert and Margaret Gisler. VGM Career Horizons, Lincolnwood, IL, 1992.

Careers for Dreamers and Doers: A Guide to Management Careers in the Nonprofit Sector. Lilly Cohen and Dennis R. Young. The Foundation Center, New York, NY, 1989.

Describes employment opportunities, includes career profiles, and provides job-hunting tips. Includes a list of associations involved in career advancement and professional development, as well as a United Way summary of position classifications and foundation position definitions. Bibliography. Indexed.

Careers for Good Samaritans and Other Humanitarian Types. Marjorie Ebert and Margaret Gisler. VGM Career Horizons, Lincolnwood, IL, 1991.

Careers in Mental Health: A Guide to Helping Occupations: The Opportunities in Mental Health and How to Prepare for Them. Paul Schmolling, Jr., William R. Burger, and Merrill Youkeles. Garrett Park Press, Garrett Park, MD, 1986.
Provides an overview, along with descriptions of specific mental health careers and work settings. Includes a chapter on self-assessment. Lists resources.

Doing Well By Doing Good: The First Complete Guide to Careers in the Nonprofit Sector. Terry W. McAdam. The Taft Group, Washington, DC, 1988.
Describes the sector and the job-search process, including the decision to accept or reject an offer. Includes case studies and sources of additional information.

Finding a Job in the Nonprofit Sector. The Taft Group, Rockville, MD, 1991.

Foundation and Corporate Giving. The Taft Group, Rockville, MD, annual.

The Foundation Directory. The Foundation Center, New York, NY, annual.
Provides information on the nation's largest foundations. The subject and type of support (for example, "grants to individuals") indexes are quite useful. Identifies publicly accessible reference collections throughout the U.S.

Foundation Grants to Individuals, 8th edition. The Foundation Center, New York, NY, 1993.
Lists foundation grant programs for individuals (as opposed to those aimed at institutional support). Foundation, subject, types of support, geographic focus, company employee grant, and specific educational institutional indexes.

Goodworks: A Guide to Careers in Social Change, 3rd edition. Joan Anzalone, editor. Dembner NY Barricade Books, New York, NY, 1985.
Information on 600 social change groups and internship and volunteer opportunities with them. Profiles on individuals in the field and additional sources of information. Geographic and topical indexes.

Great Careers: The Fourth of July Guide to Careers, Internships, and Volunteer Opportunities in the Nonprofit Sector. Devon Cottrell Smith, editor. Garrett Park Press, Garrett Park, MD, 1990.
Lists resources and organizations by topic/career area from animal rights to women's issues. Includes essays on various issues associated with work in the not-for-profit sector. Chapter indexes and general index of resources and organizations.

Handel's National Directory for the Performing Arts, 4th edition. NDPA, Inc., Dallas, TX, 1988. 2 volumes.

Volume 1 lists organizations and facilities geographically, and is indexed by arts area (dance, instrumental music, vocal music, theater, performing series, facility). Volume 2 lists educational institutions geographically, with dance, music, and theater indexes. Each volume also has a general index.

Invest Yourself: A Catalogue of Volunteer Opportunities. Susan G. Angus, editorial coordinator. Commission on Voluntary Service and Action, New York, NY, 1991.

Alphabetical listings of agencies, with indexes indicating summer and international/intercultural opportunities, as well as work camps and categories of skills and interests needed. Arranged in five sections: literary arts, media arts, multidisciplinary arts, performing arts, and visual arts. Awards, organization, geographic, and artistic discipline indexes. Includes artist-in-residence programs. Use this as a guide to employment opportunities in the foundation world as well as for sources of income to support arts projects.

Managing a Non Profit Organization. Thomas Wolf, Prentice Hall, Englewood Cliffs, NJ, 1990.

National Directory of Arts Internships. Warren Christensen, editor. National Network for Artist Placement, Los Angeles, CA, biennial.

Listings in all areas of the arts. Good introductory section on developing an internship, with practical advice on cover letters, resumes, portfolios, etc.

National Directory of Children, Youth and Family Services. Marion L. Peterson. Longmont, CO, annual.

Part 1 is a state-by-state listing of public and private services and agencies. Part 2 lists federal and national organizations and clearinghouses. Part 3 is a buyer's guide to specialized services and products.

National Directory of Non Profit Organizations. The Taft Group, Washington, DC, annual.

National Directory of Private Social Agencies. Helga B. Croner. Croner Publications, Inc., Queens Village, NY, 1990, with monthly supplements.

Geographically arranged, with index of services. Very little information beyond address and telephone numbers, but it identifies some fairly obscure services.

Nonprofits' Job Finder. Daniel Lauber. Planning/Communications, River Forest, IL, 1992.

Profitable Careers in Nonprofit. William Lewis and Carol Milano. John Wiley & Sons, Inc., New York, NY, 1987.
Profiles positions within the nonprofit area and discusses the job-search process. Lists resources and professional associations. Indexed.

Research Centers Directory. Karen Hill, editor. Gale Research Inc., Detroit, MI, annual. 2 volumes.
Subject listing of nonprofit research organizations, giving information on research activities and fields, as well as publications, services, and staff size. Subject and alphabetical indexes. Updated by *New Research Centers*.

State Foundation Directories.
Directories of private foundations registered with the state as charitable, tax-exempt institutions are available for most states. These are helpful in identifying smaller foundations not accounted for in other sources like *The Foundation Directory*. *Massachusetts Grantmakers* is produced by Associated Grantmakers of Massachusetts, Inc., a statewide professional association of leading grantmakers and their partners in the nonprofit community.

Survey of Arts Administration Training. Center for Arts Administration, Graduate School of Business, University of Wisconsin-Madison and Association of Arts Administration Educators. ACA Books, New York, NY, biennial.
Profiles programs in the U.S. and Canada. Includes a list of job placement services.

Working in Foundations: Career Patterns of Women and Men. Teresa Jean Odendahl et al. The Foundation Center, New York, NY, 1985.
Written to study the status of women relative to men in the fields of philanthropy, with a useful glimpse of the world of foundation work. Discusses recruitment and career paths.

8. Science and Technology, and Health (including computers and information sciences, environmental careers, biotech and health sciences, corporate R&D)

The Business of Biotechnology: From The Bench to The Street. R. Dana Ono, editor. Butterworth Heinemann, Stoneham, MA, 1992.
An examination of the challenges and critical issues facing the biotechnology industry by a score of experts of various kinds (e.g., management, marketing, and investment specialists, regulatory experts, and scientists).

The Complete Guide to Environmental Careers. The CEIP Fund, Inc. Island Press, Washington, DC, 1989.
Provides an overview of the field, as well as chapters on specific areas of interest within the field. Includes interviews with professionals, job-search strategies, salary information, internship and volunteer ideas, and resource lists. Indexed.

Conservation Directory: A List of Organizations, Agencies, and Officials Concerned with Natural Resource Use and Management. National Wildlife Federation, Washington, DC, annual.
Includes international, national, and interstate commissions and organizations, as well as U.S. and Canadian government and citizens' groups. Lists colleges and universities, conservation/environment offices of foreign governments, additional resources, etc. Subject and name indexes.

Directory of American Research and Technology: Organizations Active in Product Development for Business. R.R. Bowker, New York, NY, annual.
Alphabetical listing of nongovernment facilities involved in research and development, including subsidiaries. Information on staff and research fields. Geographic, personnel, and classified indexes.

The Directory of Massachusetts High Technology Companies. Mass Tech Times, Inc., Watertown, MA, annual.
Lists manufacturing, research, engineering, consulting, and software firms. Names key personnel. Product, software applications, staff size, and geographic indexes.

Encyclopedia of Medical Organizations and Agencies, 2nd edition. Anthony T. Kruzas, Kay Gill, and Robert Wilson, editors. Gale Research Co., Detroit, MI, 1987.
"A Subject Guide to More than 11,000 Medical Societies, Professional and Voluntary Associations, Foundations, Research Institutes, Federal and State Agencies, Medical and Allied Health Schools, Information Centers, Data Base Services, and Related Health Care Organizations." Master name and keyword index.

Gale Environmental Sourcebook, 1st edition. Karen Hill and Annette Piccirelli, editors. Gale Research Inc., Detroit, MI, 1992.
Comprehensive guide to public and private organizations, agencies, research centers, programs, publications (including newsletters and databases), corporate contacts, and other resources that study, define, and report on the environment. Organized by type of resource. Alphabetical and subject indexes.

Health Career Planning: A Realistic Guide. Ellen Lederman. Human Sciences Press, Inc., New York, NY, 1988.
   Focusing on the allied health fields, this book opens with a chapter on the decision-making process, then proceeds to a discussion of the student years, first years on the job, career development, stress on the job, and career change. Indexed.

The High-Tech Career Book: Finding Your Place in Today's Job Market. Betsy A. Collard. Crisp Publications, Inc., Los Altos, CA, 1986.
   An excellent guide to the high-tech field. Examines types of organizations, as well as functional areas (engineering, marketing, sales, writing, public relations). Gives practical advice on the job-search process and profiles industries and trends. Resource list, glossary, index.

High-Tech Jobs for Non-Tech Grads. Mark O'Brien. Prentice Hall, Inc., Englewood Cliffs, NJ, 1986.
   Strategies for identifying and gaining nontechnical employment in high-tech companies. Includes brief sketches of some high-tech fields and some case studies.

National Health Directory. Aspen Systems Corp., Rockville, MD, annual.
   Identifies policymakers in federal and state agencies, as well as city and county health officials. Name indexes.

New England Directory for Computer Professionals. The Bradford Co., Scituate, MA, annual.
   Alphabetical listing of companies with MIS/DP departments. Identifies DP managers and systems/computers on site. Geographic index.

Peterson's Job Opportunities for Engineering, Science, and Computer Graduates. Peterson's Guides, Princeton, NJ, annual.
   Contains profiles of selected employers, and has an excellent resource section. Includes starting location, internship, summer job, training program, and other special interest indexes.

State-by-State Biotechnology Directory: Centers, Companies, and Contacts. Biotechnology Information Division of the North Carolina Biotechnology Center. The Bureau of National Affairs, Inc., Washington, DC, 1990.
   Geographically lists state government contacts, nonprofit research centers, and companies actually working with new technologies. Lists some federal contacts. Company index.

World Environmental Directory, North America, 5th edition. Business Publishers Inc., Silver Spring, MD, 1989.
Lists companies, agencies, and organizations, including attorneys with environmental interests, corporate environmental officials, educational institutions, and grants. Separate sections for international and Canadian organizations. Personnel index.